Grading Exceptional

AND

Struggling Learners

LEE ANN JUNG

THOMAS R. GUSKEY

CORWIN
A SAGE Company

CORWIN
A SAGE Company

FOR INFORMATION:

Corwin

A SAGE Company

2455 Teller Road

Thousand Oaks, California 91320

(800) 233-9936

Fax: (800) 417-2466

www.corwin.com

SAGE Ltd.

1 Oliver's Yard

55 City Road

London, EC1Y 1SP

United Kingdom

SAGE Pvt. Ltd.

B 1/I 1 Mohan Cooperative Industrial Area

Mathura Road, New Delhi 110 044

India

SAGE Asia-Pacific Pte. Ltd.

33 Pekin Street #02-01

Far East Square

Singapore 048763

Acquisitions Editor: Dan Alpert
Associate Editor: Megan Bedell
Editorial Assistant: Sarah Bartlett
Project Editor: Veronica Stapleton
Copy Editor: Cate Huisman
Typesetter: Hurix
Proofreader: Dennis W. Webb
Indexer: Molly Hall
Cover Designer: Michael Dubowe
Permissions Editor: Karen Ehrmann

Printed in the United States of America

Jung, Lee Ann.
Grading exceptional and struggling learners / Lee Ann Jung and Thomas R. Guskey.

p. cm.
Includes bibliographical references and index.

ISBN 978-1-4129-8833-9 (pbk.)
1. Learning disabled children. 2. Grading and marking (Students) I. Guskey, Thomas R. II. Title.

LC4704.J86 2012 371.9—dc23 2011033249

This book is printed on acid-free paper.

14 15 16 17 18 10 9 8 7 6 5 4 3 2

Contents

About the Authors

Lee Ann Jung, PhD, is an associate professor of special education at the University of Kentucky. She entered the field of special education in 1994 and has worked as a teacher, administrator, and researcher. Dr. Jung has authored more than 30 peer-reviewed journal articles and book chapters and is an editorial board member for several special education journals. She has been awarded more than $3 million in federal and state funding to support personnel preparation and research at the university. Her work is used by numerous early intervention and special education programs. She is a frequent national presenter and consultant on the development of individualized education plans (IEPs) and individualized family service plans (IFSPs), intervention planning, progress monitoring, and consultative service delivery. Dr. Jung is a 2001 graduate of Auburn University. She can be reached by e-mail at ljung@uky.edu.

Kari Maloney Photography and Design (http://www.karimaloneyphoto.com/index.html)

Thomas R. Guskey, PhD, is professor of educational psychology in the College of Education at the University of Kentucky. A graduate of the University of Chicago, he began his career in education as a middle school teacher, served as an administrator in the Chicago Public Schools, and was the first director of the Center for the Improvement of Teaching and Learning, a national educational research center. He is the author of numerous award-winning books and over 200 articles and papers. Dr. Guskey served on the policy research team of the National Commission on Teaching and America's Future and on the task force of the National Staff Development Council that developed the national standards for professional development, and he has been named a fellow in the American Educational Research Association; this is one of the association's highest honors. He coedits the Experts in Assessment Series for Corwin and has been featured on the National Public Radio programs "Talk of the Nation" and "Morning Edition." He can be reached by e-mail at Guskey@uky.edu.

1

The Challenges of Grading Struggling Learners

The day report cards are sent home is one filled with anticipation and excitement for some students but anxiety and fear for many others. All of us can recall at least one report card day when concerns about whether or not we made the "cutoff" for a particular grade kept us from concentrating on our schoolwork. The process of grading can be such a mystery to students that often they have no idea what will appear on their report card until it arrives. And because teachers vary so much in the procedures they use for determining students' grades, the more teachers a student has, the more complicated the reporting process becomes.

For struggling learners, the uncertainty over grades can be especially distressing. Widespread inconsistencies in the way teachers determine the grades assigned to struggling learners make interpretation nearly impossible. Even if a teacher has a predetermined formula for determining grades, that formula can be different for each struggling learner in the class. Furthermore, because teachers often decide how they will grade struggling learners at the *end* of the grading period instead of at the beginning, the grades assigned are not only difficult to interpret but impossible to predict.

Of course, many teachers feel just as anxious as their students on report card day. Teacher preparation programs seldom include course work or even discussions of recommended practices for grading students in general, much less for students who may be struggling learners. As a result, teachers at all grade levels grapple with issues of fairness in grading, especially with regard to students who are struggling. Some of the most troubling questions they face include these:

- What grade do I give a student with a disability who has given excellent effort but did not meet the standards?
- Is it fair to give a passing grade to an English learner who did not pass the grade-level language standards?
- What do I do about the grade for the student who I suspect has a disability and is receiving intensive intervention through a Response to Intervention (RTI) model but has not been diagnosed?
- How can I ensure that the grades that I assign to all students are both fair and accurate?

Questions like these about fairness and appropriateness surface every time teachers have to complete report cards. Assigning fair report card grades to struggling learners is an even more daunting problem. Although struggling learners compose only about 20% of students, this problem affects 100% of teachers (Jung & Guskey, 2010a).

Despite the magnitude of this problem, few recommendations for grading struggling learners can be found in the research literature or in education policy. In the absence of thoughtful and consistent guidance from researchers, policy makers, or school leaders, teachers are left on their own to solve the problem. As a result, the approaches they develop vary widely, even among teachers within the same school. Most unfortunate is the fact that their approaches typically lack both fairness and accuracy. Even when teachers recognize that their practices may not be fair or accurate, they usually have no idea of where to turn for information about better or more effective alternatives.

In this context, the frustration for parents of struggling learners comes as no surprise. One of the most important functions of grades and report cards is to give families information on their children's progress in school. Families want and need to know their children's academic strengths, the areas where the children are experiencing difficulty, and what they can do at home to promote success. Yet most parents of struggling learners feel that grades and report cards give them little if any meaningful information. Occasionally the progress report that accompanies the report card offers them a portion of the information that they need. But more often than not, even individualized progress reports lack the clear, concise, and detailed information that families want and hope to receive.

Who Are "Exceptional" or "Struggling" Learners?

In this book, we use the words *exceptional* and *struggling* to describe several groups of students. For our purposes, the category of "exceptional or struggling learners" includes students who are English learners, those who have disabilities, and those receiving intensive intervention through an RTI model. Although we focus on these three categories of learners, the practices that we describe and the model for grading we will present apply to *all* students who are struggling, whether or not they qualify for any type of special services.

Because most struggling students fall into one of these three categories, let's review the criteria for a student to qualify for each and some snapshot examples. The four student snapshots presented below represent common grading challenges teachers face. We will return to these same examples throughout the book to illustrate specific applications of the grading policies and practices we will introduce. These snapshots represent students who are struggling in school for different reasons and at various grade levels. Each of these students has unique strengths as well as specific areas that need support. All are experiencing difficulties in meeting grade-level standards.

English Learners

One category of struggling learners includes students for whom English is not their primary language and who have limited skills in reading, writing, speaking, and listening to English. Students classified as English learners (ELs) make up approximately 10% of the prekindergarten through 12th-grade population in the United States (Gotlieb, 2006). About two thirds of the EL population is elementary aged (Gotlieb, 2006), and, thus, many are not only developing English skills but are *dual language learners*, still learning the primary language spoken in their homes. ELs often have difficulty across all subject areas until they gain some minimal level of proficiency with the English language. The challenges these students face in language arts can persist for years. Reporting their level of proficiency relative to subject-area standards during the time they are mastering grade-level English language skills poses major challenges for teachers. In addition, understanding the meaning of the grades assigned to ELs can be particularly confusing for their parents, who also may have limited English language skills.

SNAPSHOT: Carlos

Carlos is a fifth-grade English learner who moved to the United States from Puerto Rico five months ago. Because his family speaks very little English, he has few English language models at home. Carlos was very quiet and shy during his first few months at school but has since gained an excellent command of conversational English and has become friends with several boys in his class. Carlos's skills in conversation, however, far surpass his English language skills in the academic setting. He has great difficulty with written English and, thus, is not on grade level in any academic subject. His vocabulary is at approximately a second-grade level. Although he struggles with English, Carlos is a very dedicated and hard-working student. He does his best to complete assignments but often appears frustrated because of his difficulties in understanding the language.

Students With Disabilities

A second category of struggling learners is students who have disabilities and qualify for special education services through the Individuals With Disabilities Education Act (IDEIA, 2004). We also refer to these students as *exceptional* learners. By fifth grade, nearly 12% of students in the United States receive some form of special education services (Herring, McGrath, & Buckley, 2006). Furthermore, the amount of time students with disabilities spend in general education classes has increased dramatically in recent years (Data Accountability Center, n.d.). As a result, nearly every classroom teacher today must face the instructional challenges presented by these students, and they have little guidance or direction from special education experts. Although there is a wealth of research indicating the positive effects of including students with disabilities in regular education classrooms (e.g., Baker, Wang, & Walberg, 1995; Carlberg & Kavale, 1980; Hunt, Farron-Davis, Beckstead, Curtis, & Goetz, 1994; Waldron, 1998), the process poses significant difficulties with regard to grading and reporting on the performance of these students. It is little wonder that reporting on the progress of students with disabilities is the IDEA requirement for individualized education programs (IEPs) that states have the greatest difficulty meeting (Etscheidt, 2006).

The most common category of disability is specific learning disability. Learning disability (LD) is a neurological disorder that causes difficulty with academic performance. Students with LD may have trouble with any number of academic tasks, including reading, writing, organizing information, solving problems, or recalling information. A common misconception is that individuals with learning disabilities have lower than average intelligence. But individuals with learning disabilities often have IQs far above average (Horowitz, 2006). Nearly 2.5 million U.S. students receive special education for learning disability (Data Accountability Center, n.d.), meaning most teachers will have several students in every class each year who have this exceptionality.

SNAPSHOT: Janis

Janis is a 10th-grade student in an urban school district who qualifies for special education because of a specific learning disability in the area of written expression. Janis entered special education in third grade after her parents and teachers became concerned about slow progress in her reading fluency, comprehension, and writing skills. Although her reading pace is still slow, intervention has improved Janis's reading comprehension dramatically. She is still working to improve her skills in writing. When given the opportunity to express her knowledge orally, Janis performs at or above her grade level in all subject areas. Her written responses have steadily improved but currently are at approximately a seventh-grade level. Janis struggles with the mechanics of writing as well as expressing her thoughts fully and clearly when writing. Janis receives intervention targeting her writing within the general education classroom as well as in the special education classroom for one hour each day.

Some students who qualify for special education have moderate or severe disabilities and often qualify based on diagnosed medical condition(s). Such students tend to be significantly behind their classmates in several or all subject areas. Completing a traditional report card for students with significant disabilities can be especially problematic for teachers. Most consider it unfair to assign failing grades to students with moderate or severe disabilities who try hard but still are unable to demonstrate proficiency on grade-level standards.

Furthermore, legal provisions require that IEPs written for children with disabilities enable them "to achieve passing marks and advance from grade to grade" (*Board of Education v. Rowley*, 1982, pp. 187–204). From a legal perspective, a failing grade shows that appropriate educational services were *not* provided. At the same time, assigning passing marks to students who have not yet met grade-level performance standards also seems inappropriate, because it inaccurately portrays such students' actual level of achievement. For these reasons, the parents of children with moderate to severe disabilities rarely find the report card to be informative or useful.

SNAPSHOT: Jimi

Jimi is an eighth-grade student who qualifies for special education because he has been diagnosed with Down syndrome. He enjoys being with his friends in the general education class and his special education class. Jimi spends three hours each day in the general education classroom and three hours each day in a special education classroom. In addition to academic interventions, Jimi also receives occupational therapy and speech therapy to support his fine motor, oral motor, and speech development. Those who know Jimi can understand his speech, but others have some difficulty understanding his words completely. Jimi is learning to read and currently is able to read books at the kindergarten and first-grade levels with help. He is developing the ability to write and can write his name without help. Jimi's skills in mathematics include the ability to sort, group, and count. He is beginning to add with objects. Jimi enjoys reading and mathematics with objects, but he does not like writing.

Students Receiving Intensive Intervention

The final category of struggling learner we will discuss is students who are struggling enough to require intensive intervention, often within an RTI framework. RTI is a set of assessment and intervention practices that allows teachers to identify early those students who may have individual learning difficulties and then to address those difficulties directly with effective instructional strategies (Mellard & Johnson, 2008). For some students, a short period of intensive intervention remedies the difficulties, and no further special services are needed. For others, long-term intensive intervention is needed to maintain sufficient progress.

As they do with the other categories of struggling learners, teachers may feel confused about how to assign grades to a student who is receiving intensive intervention. Although the student may not be meeting grade-level standards, most teachers may find it difficult to assign a failing grade to a student who is putting forth extraordinary effort and making excellent progress. How can we communicate with a single grade that a student is struggling and needs additional help but also is trying hard and making significant improvement?

SNAPSHOT: Norah

Norah is a second-grade student who is experiencing difficulty in the area of reading fluency and decoding. Despite her difficulty with fluency, her reading comprehension is excellent. Norah's school, using an RTI model, is offering extra reading instruction to Norah. She is receiving direct instruction in a small group with other struggling readers three times each week for an hour; she also receives individual direct instruction twice each week for 30 minutes. Her reading specialist is using a curriculum-based measure to track her progress weekly. Norah's reading level is about one grade level behind, and she is still considered at risk. But since she began daily reading intervention, her skills have steadily improved.

Common Solutions

Although the students like those described in the snapshots above are exceptional, they are by no means rare. As we described earlier, struggling learners are estimated to make up approximately 20% of the student population. As a result, every classroom teacher today faces the challenge of grading struggling learners. For those students who receive most or all of their supports and services in a general education classroom, the general education teacher typically takes responsibility for assigning grades on the regular report card. Specialists such as special education teachers or EL teachers typically report on progress toward IEP, EL, or other individualized goals in a separate progress report that accompanies the report card. Although this seems a logical division of labor, it leaves the general education teacher without help in deciding the appropriate grade to assign these students in each content area.

Lacking explicit recommendations on grading, most general education teachers make individual, informal grading adaptations for struggling learners (Polloway et al., 1994). In recent years, researchers have recommended a variety of such adaptations to better meet individual students' needs (Silva, Munk, & Bursuck, 2005). The adaptations they recommend for struggling learners generally fall into one of five broad categories:

1. Grading on individualized goals

2. Grading based on improvement over past performance

3. Weighting assignments differently

4. Including indicators of effort or behavior in the grade

5. Modifying the grading scale (Silva et al., 2005).

Let's consider each of these adaptations and its specific implications.

Grading on Individualized Goals

One of the most common approaches to grading struggling learners is to assign a grade based on the student's individualized goals. These individual goals may be stated in the IEP or EL plan. For students receiving RTI, they may be less formal. Individualized goals are usually based on a team's assessment of the student's general skills and often are not directly connected to curriculum standards.

Teachers approach this type of adaptation in many different ways. An A in language arts on Jimi's report card, for example, could mean that he exceeded his IEP goal for articulation in verbal communication. Although the teacher may have followed a logical process to arrive at this grade, Jimi's parents would likely have difficulty appropriately interpreting this grade without additional explanation from the teacher.

Similarly, Norah's report card might indicate a B in language arts. For Norah, that could mean that even though she is still behind her grade level, she met the goals set for her by a reading specialist. If Norah meets those goals and on that basis receives all As and Bs in language arts, but then is referred for special education, her parents are likely to be both surprised and confused.

Grading Based on Improvement Over Past Performance

A second type of adaptation is to base the report card grade on the degree of improvement since the last reporting period. Carlos, for example, may make incredible strides in his English language acquisition from the first reporting period to the second. It is completely understandable that his teacher would want to acknowledge that progress with a high grade in language arts, even if Carlos is not yet meeting the standards expected for his grade level. It hardly seems fair to assign a failing grade to a student showing such progress amidst difficult circumstances. But how is Carlos's family to understand what he has achieved? If grades are based on progress alone, parents are unable to know what skills their children have acquired or where they stand in terms of grade-level expectations.

Weighting Assignments Differently

Another option for adapting grades is to weight assignments differently for students who are struggling from the way they are weighted for other students in the class. Homework and assignments completed as a group, for example, might be given more weight for struggling learners, while major assessments and assignments completed individually by students in class are given less weight. For Carlos, weighting homework and group assignments more heavily could change his report card grade in science from a D to a B. His teacher may feel better about assigning the B to Carlos, especially since he is an English learner. But she also must realize that this grade is not an accurate reflection of Carlos's true performance in science. Looking at only the report card, Carlos appears to be achieving the same as the other students in his class who are actually on grade level.

Including Indicators of Behavior or Effort in the Grade

Considering a student's behavior or effort in the grade is also a common adaptation for struggling learners. But this again results in a clouding of the meaning of the grade and makes it impossible to understand what the student has actually learned and is able to do. Furthermore, because teachers vary in how much they count behavior or effort, it is possible that Jimi's A is based entirely upon his behavior, but Janis's C is calculated by weighting effort 50% and achievement 50%. The grade alone gives no meaningful information on how effort was included.

Modifying the Grading Scale

The simplest way to adapt grades for students who are struggling is to alter the grading scale mathematically so that the percentage or points required to earn each grade is lower. In Carlos's class, for example, grading may be based on a traditional percentage scale, where 90% to 100% is an A, 80% to 89% is a B, and so forth. For Janis, however, it may be decided that because of her learning disability, a modified percentage scale is more appropriate. So for Janis, each grade cut-off is set 10% lower. With that adaptation, an A for Janis would be 80% or greater, a B 70% to 79%, a C 60% to 69%, and so forth. This adapted grading scale makes it more likely that Janis will receive a passing grade. But Janis is also a high school student, and the grades recorded on her transcript will be viewed by the colleges or places of employment to which she applies. Because the transcript will not include the grading scale that was used for each class, those who look to her transcript for information on her performance will be receiving distorted information.

Problems With Grading Adaptations

For each of the struggling learners in our examples, the above grading adaptations would all result in higher report card grades. Unfortunately, that is also the *only* outcome of adapting grades in these ways. These new grades are not necessarily accurate nor do they offer better information about a student's true academic performance. Because individual grading adaptations change the ruler by which students' performance is measured, understanding the meaning of adapted grades is impossible. Does an A mean that the student met criteria? Or does it mean the student demonstrated high effort? Maybe the A means the student participated well. The grade may be some combination of all of these factors and maybe others.

A primary reason that teachers adapt grades is they believe adjustments that make higher grades attainable will encourage struggling learners to try even harder (Silva et al., 2005). In addition, these adaptations provide students who are unable to meet grade-level standards with the opportunity to earn higher grades, which seems only fair. But in reality, these adapted grades can lead such students to believe that their grades are the result of who they are, not what they do. This, in turn, leads to *decreased* student motivation (Ring & Reetz, 2000). Grading adaptations also introduce issues of injustice to other students who, along with many of their teachers, feel that adapted grades are inappropriate and unfair (Bursuck, Munk, & Olson, 1999). Furthermore, even with these adaptations, most struggling learners continue to receive low passing grades, placing them at high risk for low self-esteem and for dropping out of school (Donahue & Zigmond, 1990).

Summary

Teachers desperately need new ways to communicate accurate information about the performance of struggling learners. They want to ensure that parents and others can understand that information and can use it for decision making. But they also want ways to provide that information that are practical and efficient and that do not create a bookkeeping nightmare for teachers.

In the next chapter we will discuss grading processes and practices that allow teachers to do just that. We will show how relatively modest changes in grading procedures can help teachers resolve many of these dilemmas. We also will show how changes in the format of the report card will solve many reporting problems and allow teachers to communicate more accurate and honest information without increasing their already burdensome record-keeping tasks.

2

A Foundation for Change

In the first chapter we introduced some of the challenges associated with grading exceptional or struggling learners, particularly those who are English learners, those who have disabilities, and those identified for intensive intervention through a Response to Intervention (RTI) model. These challenges make clear the need for grading procedures that communicate accurate information about students' performance in school and that can be easily understood by students, parents, and others. Such procedures must be direct, unambiguous, honest, and fair. At the same time, they also need to be efficient and easy to implement so that they do not overload teachers with burdensome bookkeeping tasks.

In developing these procedures, it is important to keep in mind that their quality will be limited by the quality of the grading system in place for *all* students. So in this chapter we turn our attention to foundational elements that must be in place within a school's grading and reporting system in order to ensure that all students receive grades that are accurate, meaningful, and fair. We then describe additional elements that need to be in place when assigning grades to struggling learners.

Breaking Tradition

On most traditional report cards, students receive a single letter grade or percentage for each subject or course that is a part of their instructional program. Most teachers are comfortable with this type of reporting, because it is the same as they experienced as students. Most parents like it as well for the same reason. It is also the basis of nearly all of the computerized grading programs available to educators today. Teachers and parents favor this type of reporting because they believe they know what an A means, what a B means, and so forth. But are we really able to make judgments about a student's performance based on these letter grades or percentages? And if so, how accurate are our judgments? Consider, for example, the grades assigned below for the students we described in the snapshots presented in Chapter 1:

Carlos	
Language Arts	B
Mathematics	B
Science	A
Social Studies	A

Janis	
Language Arts	C
Mathematics	D
Science	C
Social Studies	B

Jimi	
Language Arts	A
Mathematics	A
Science	A
Social Studies	A

Norah	
Language Arts	A
Mathematics	A
Science	A
Social Studies	A

Looking at these grades, most people would conclude they know a lot about the performance of Carlos, Janis, Jimi, and Norah. It appears that Jimi and Norah are both outstanding students, Carlos is doing fairly well, and Janis is struggling, especially in mathematics. But is that really true?

Carlos's B in language arts, for example, could mean many different things. Perhaps Carlos did not master any of the grade-level language arts standards that he was expected to learn during the marking period, but he displayed a great deal of effort and completed his homework every day. In fact, any of the common grading adaptations presented in Chapter 1 could have been used to determine Carlos's grade. And if so, we really know very little about what Carlos's B truly means.

Janis's report card is equally confusing. She received low but passing grades in several subjects and appears to be doing satisfactory work in social studies. Janis may have received low grades in language arts, mathematics, and science because she did not meet grade-level standards in these subjects. But students with learning disabilities frequently have difficulty with organizational skills. So it might be the case that Janis actually did quite well and met the standards in these subjects, but forgot to bring homework assignments back to school and, as a result, received lower grades.

Similarly, it is impossible to discern precisely what Jimi learned and is able to do. Recall, Jimi has a significant disability. He may not have met the grade-level standards in any subject but received high grades due to his exceptional effort. Still, based on the information included in the report card, no one can tell what he accomplished, what strengths he has, or what he is ready to begin next. In fact, anyone who saw Jimi's report card not knowing his background information would assume that he met or exceeded the grade-level standards in every subject.

Norah's report card is just as misleading as Jimi's. We know that Norah struggles in language arts and has been identified for intensive intervention. Yet her grade for language arts is an A. If Norah does not respond adequately to the intervention, her teacher will probably have difficulty explaining to her parents and to other teachers why Norah is being referred for special education even though she earned As in all subjects.

The tradition of assigning a single letter grade or percentage to students for each subject or course included on the report card requires teachers to combine numerous diverse sources of evidence into one mark. This results in a hodgepodge grade that includes some combination of achievement, behavior, effort, attitude, and learning progress (Cizek, Fitzgerald, & Rachor, 1996; McMillan, 2001; McMillan, Myran, & Workman, 2002). Even when teachers identify the weighting strategies they use to combine these diverse elements and use computerized grading programs to ensure accuracy in their computations, the final grade remains a confusing amalgam that is impossible to interpret and rarely presents a true picture of a student's academic proficiency (Brookhart, 1991, Cross & Frary, 1996; Guskey, 2002b). In short, a single letter grade for a subject or course is insufficient and ineffective for communicating how *any* student is performing in school.

A New Foundation

Although combining indicators of achievement, behavior, and learning progress creates a meaningless hodgepodge grade, information on each of these types of criteria remains an important part of a high-quality grading and reporting system. Especially for struggling learners, families want to know about their children's attitudes, effort, participation, conduct, and other nonacademic factors. This kind of information can offer key clues about the appropriateness of interventions and the placement selected.

Carlos, for example, may participate differently in oral reading tasks when in a group of other English learners than he does in the general education class. Janis, on the other hand, may show greater effort in the general education classroom than she does in her resource room. In addition to his academic performance, Jimi's parents may want to know how he is getting along with other students in his class. Although social skills are not a part of the school report card, they are an important part of his individualized education program (IEP). And Norah's parents may want to know if her grade reflects her performance relative to grade-level standards or simply the progress she has made since becoming involved in the intervention.

Distinguish Learning Goals

Since information about both academic and nonacademic factors is important but disguised when combined into a single grade or mark, the simplest solution is to report information on these various factors separately. There is nothing sacred or even particularly useful about assigning a single grade or mark for each academic subject on the report card. In fact, standards-based reporting compels teachers to break down each subject or course into more specific standards or strands of standards and then to report students' performance on each separately. The same can be done when reporting on nonacademic factors.

Most curriculum frameworks describe specific academic learning standards or goals. These form the core of every school's curriculum and are the basis of most teachers' instructional planning. But as we noted earlier, teachers frequently consider goals other than those associated strictly with cognitive or academic areas when assigning grades or marks. These other goals often relate to student behavior in school and are associated with traits such as responsibility, citizenship, cooperation, respect, and effort. Occasionally such goals have to do with students' work habits and consider things such as completion of homework, class participation, punctuality in turning in assignments, or the appearance and neatness of students' work.

The different learning goals that teachers consider in grading can generally be classified into three broad categories (see Guskey,

2004, 2006b; Guskey & Bailey, 2001). These categories, in turn, correspond to three distinct types of reporting standards. They include *product*, *process*, and *progress* goals.

1. **Product Goals** describe the major cognitive and academic learning outcomes being sought. They provide the foundation for standards-based reporting as well as for all standards-based approaches to teaching and learning (Stiggins, 2008). Product goals center on *what* students should know and be able to do at a particular point in time. Grades or marks based on product goals are usually determined from the results of students' performance on summative examinations; final products such as reports, projects, or exhibits; overall assessments; and other culminating demonstrations of learning.

2. **Process Goals** focus on classroom behaviors and activities that enable learning, rather than on specific learning outcomes. They derive from the belief that grading and reporting should reflect not just the final results but also *how* students achieved them. In other words, process goals consider what students do in order to reach the product goals. Some researchers consider these goals to be "enabling" behaviors or traits (McMillan, 2001). Responsibility, effort, study skills, work habits, homework completion and quality, class participation, and punctuality in turning in assignments would all be considered process goals. So too would be the results from formative assessments and other checks on student learning designed primarily to guide teachers and students in identifying and then correcting of learning difficulties.

3. **Progress Goals** consider how much students actually gain from their learning experiences. They relate not necessarily to where students are relative to standards or product goals, but to how much improvement has been made over a particular period of time. Other names for progress goals include *learning gain, value-added learning,* and *educational growth and development.* For struggling learners, progress goals are often articulated within individualized plans, such as an English learner (EL) plan, an IEP, or a less-formalized plan in the case of students receiving intensive intervention in an RTI model. For students with disabilities, schools are required to report on progress toward IEP goals at least as often as they send home reports for all children—so as often as report cards are sent home (IDEIA, 2004). Many schools extend the same practice to include English learners and other students who have individualized progress goals. Parents of struggling learners depend on high-quality progress information to make informed decisions about placement and direction for intervention.

Some educators distinguish between *progress,* which they measure backward from a final performance standard or goal, and *growth,* which is measured forward from the place a student begins on a learning continuum (e.g., Wiggins, 1996). We believe, however, that if improvement is judged on the basis of well-defined and credible learning standards that include graduated levels of performance or a specified learning progression, progress and growth can be considered synonymous.

Because progress goals focus on how far students have come over a particular period of time, grades or marks based on progress goals can be highly individualized among students. Most of the current research evidence on progress goals comes from studies of students involved in individually or differentially paced instructional programs (Esty & Teppo, 1992) and those involved in certain special education services that might include an IEP (Gersten, Vaughn, & Brengelman, 1996; Ring & Reetz, 2000).

Types of Learning Goals Used in Reporting

1. *Product* Goals
2. *Process* Goals
3. *Progress* Goals

When compelled to assign a single grade for each subject or course, most teachers combine evidence related to all three of these types of learning goals (Brookhart, 1993; Frary, Cross, & Weber, 1993; Friedman & Manley, 1992; Nava & Loyd, 1992; Stiggins, Frisbie, & Griswold, 1989). Many do so because of concerns about student motivation, self-esteem, and the social consequences of grading and reporting. Studies indicate that teachers also vary the particular goals they consider from student to student, taking into account individual circumstances or special needs (Bursuck et al., 1996; Natriello, Riehl, & Pallas, 1994; Truog & Friedman, 1996). Although they do this in an effort to be fair, it makes interpreting the grade impossible, not only for families, but also for administrators, community members, and even the students themselves (Friedman & Frisbie, 1995; Jung & Guskey, 2010a; Waltman & Frisbie, 1994). A high grade or mark, for example, might mean the student mastered all of the standards before instruction began (product), did not achieve as well as expected but tried very hard (process), or simply made significant improvement during the time considered (progress).

Dilemmas Posed by Different Learning Goals

Recognizing the interpretation problems posed by combining evidence related to these different types of learning goals, especially when assigning grades to struggling learners, most researchers and measurement specialists recommend the exclusive use of product goals in determining the grades or marks assigned to students' performance. They point out that the more process and progress elements come into play, the more subjective and biased grades can become (Ornstein, 1994). How can a teacher know, for example, how difficult a task was for a student or how hard that student worked to complete it?

Many teachers point out, however, that basing grades or marks on product goals only would allow some high-ability students to receive high grades with little effort, while the hard work of struggling learners may go unacknowledged.

Consider, for example, the case of Norah, the second-grade student we described in Chapter 1 who is struggling in the area of reading fluency. Another student in Norah's class is an accomplished reader and fluently reads books on a third-grade level without assistance. Nevertheless, this student seldom displays any effort while reading and often appears uncooperative. Norah, on the other hand, consistently puts forth extraordinary effort during reading instruction, always tries hard, and displays a kind and cooperative disposition during all reading tasks. Yet despite her efforts, Norah is unable to perform at the same level as her fluently reading but uncooperative classmate.

Few teachers would consider it fair to use only product goals related to grade-level standards in language arts in determining the grades assigned to these two students (see Guskey & Bailey, 2001, 2010). If that were the case, Norah would receive a failing grade or mark despite her hard work, while her classmate would receive a high grade. Under these conditions, struggling learners who must work hardest to meet standards have the least incentive to do so (Jung & Guskey, 2007, 2010a, 2010b). Such students find the relationship between high effort and low grades unacceptable and, as a result, often express their displeasure with indifference, deception, or disruption (Tomlinson, 1992).

Solving the Dilemmas

A practical solution to the problems associated with these different learning goals, and one used by increasing numbers of teachers and schools as they develop standards-based report cards, is to report *separate* grades or marks for students on each set of goals. In other words, after establishing explicit indicators of product, process, and progress learning goals, teachers assign separate grades or marks to each. In this way the marks representing students' performance on specific academic standards are kept distinct from those assigned to demonstrations of study skills, work habits, effort, or learning progress (Guskey, 2002a, 2006b; Stiggins, 2008). The intent is to provide a more accurate, more meaningful, and much more comprehensive picture of what students accomplish in school—especially important qualities when assigning grades to the performance of struggling learners.

In general, elementary schools are further along in the process of implementing standards-based report cards that offer separate grades or marks for product, process, and progress goals than are middle schools or high schools. This is due, at least in part, to differences in curriculum diversification at these levels. In most school districts, all 2nd-grade students are engaged in learning the same academic standards, but that is not true of all 10th-grade students who are taking different courses at different levels. These curriculum differences require different reporting formats. So while the same standards-based report card may be appropriate for all students in 2nd grade, that would not be true for all students in 10th grade.

Reporting Standards

In addition to giving separate marks on the report card for product, process, and progress learning goals, educators must also consider how many standards to include. In other words, how many academic (product) standards should be listed on the report card for each subject area at the elementary level and for each course at the secondary level? In an effort to be thorough and comprehensive, many educators make the mistake of listing far too many standards on the report card and describe those standards in way too much detail. This often occurs when report card designers use unedited state or provincial standards as a basis for their work.

Most state and provincial standards are designed to help educators plan instruction and design appropriate assessments—and they are excellent tools for these purposes. For reporting, however, state and provincial standards are typically too many in number and are not expressed in parent-friendly language. If used as a basis for designing a report card, they often create a bookkeeping nightmare for teachers, who must maintain comprehensive records for every student on each one of those standards. It also frustrates parents who struggle to make sense of so much detail. This is especially true for the parents of struggling learners, whose understanding of the grade-level or course standards is critically important.

Deciding how many standards to report in each subject area is best accomplished through a three-step process (see Guskey & Bailey, 2010). First, each standard must be categorized as reflecting a *product*, *process*, or *progress* goal. Since nearly all content and performance standards included in district, state, or provincial curriculum frameworks reflect academic achievement and fall into the product category, this rarely presents a problem. Distinguishing the specific process and progress goals considered most important can prove a bit more challenging.

Second, the exact *reporting* standards in each subject area that will be included on the report card must be identified. For product goals, this typically involves translating the highly detailed *academic content* and *performance* standards outlined in curriculum frameworks to broader and more general *reporting* standards. And third, those reporting standards must be worded in clear, precise, and parent-friendly language.

Steps in Deciding How Many Standards to Report

1. Categorize standards as reflecting *product, process,* or *progress* goals.
2. Identify specific reporting standards for each subject area.
3. Word the standards in clear, precise, and parent-friendly language.

Source: Guskey & Bailey, 2010.

In developing reporting standards, an important balance must be struck when deciding what particular standards to include in each subject area or course. Specifically, the reporting standards must offer enough information to be meaningful, but not so much that they confuse or overwhelm parents and guardians. In most cases, listing *four to six reporting standards* in each subject area or course related to product goals tends to be ideal. Fewer than four requires the blending of multiple academic elements that often confounds their meaning. More than six, however, tends to make things too complicated and much more difficult to remember. Most people can keep track of four to six elements. Seven tests the upper limit of recall, and nine is simply too many.

Limiting standards-based report cards to four to six reporting standards in each subject area or course represents a departure from nearly all standards-related documents. But if taken more as "strands" of standards, the work becomes easier and more meaningful. In addition to adhering to a manageable number of reporting standards, it is important that developers agree on reporting standards that best represent the major concepts and skills students need to master for each subject area in the curriculum.

Sample Report Cards

As we described earlier, elementary educators are generally further along in the process of developing standards-based report cards than are their secondary colleagues. Nevertheless, middle school and high school educators have made tremendous strides in standards-based reporting in recent years. The report cards developed for use at the elementary and secondary levels share many similarities but also have features that make them uniquely appropriate for each level.

Two examples of portions of standards-based reporting forms that provide separate marks for different types of learning goals are shown in Figures 2.1 and 2.2. The first is an elementary form, while the second offers a middle school or high school model. Each figure depicts the second page of a four-page report card. The first page of each includes a statement of the report card's purpose, information about the student, and information about the school. The third page would be similar to the second page, depicting standards for additional subject areas or courses. The fourth page usually displays a cumulative record of marks from previous marking periods, along with notes on additional process goals related to citizenship and school or community service.

The elementary standards in Figure 2.1 offer two sets of marks: Standard Marks (for product goals), and Process Marks (for process goals). The Standard Marks are numerals reflecting four levels of student performance with regard to that standard or area of standards. These include the following:

4 = Exemplary

3 = Proficient

2 = Progressing

1 = Struggling

N/A = Not Assessed

The Process Marks, on the other hand, are symbols indicating three levels of frequency in occurrence:

$$++ = \text{Consistently}$$
$$+ = \text{Sometimes}$$
$$- = \text{Rarely}$$
$$\text{N/A} = \text{Not Assessed}$$

These marks are explained in legends at the top of the page.

Following the legends are sections for reporting on each subject area. Each section begins with a photograph of the teacher, included simply to personalize the report card and help families become familiar with their child's teachers. In self-contained, elementary classes, this may be a single teacher. In other schools where students have one teacher for language arts and social studies and another for mathematics and science, however, multiple teachers would be included. Typically students have different teachers for art, music, and physical education as well.

Beside each teacher's photograph is listed the subject area and the reporting standards for that subject. As we described earlier, these often represent broad subdivisions or standard strands within the subject area. The language arts section, for example, is based on the *Common Core State Standards Initiative* (Council of Chief State School Officers & National Governors Association Center for Best Practices, 2010) and lists five strands of standards in language arts: Reading, Writing, Listening, Speaking, and Language. Parents who want more detailed information about what aspect of the standard was the focus of instruction during a particular marking period can refer to online curriculum documents that describe those specific details.

Beside the Standard Goals are listed the Process Goals teachers assessed during the marking period. These particular process elements (Preparation, Participation, Homework, Cooperation, and Respect) are not the only ones that could have been considered. They simply represent those believed most important by the educators who developed this form. Parents who want more precise information about the criteria used in assigning the marks for these Process Goals can find those in an online reference guide as well.

Also included is a section for Descriptions and Comments, where teachers can enter two or three sentences further clarifying the focus of instruction in that subject area during the marking period, along with comments about the learning progress of individual students. For struggling learners, this is where teachers can offer more detailed information about students' unique strengths and areas where additional work may be needed.

The Mathematics section lists six broad standard strands representing Operations and Algebraic Thinking, Number and Operations—Base Ten, Number and Operations—Fractions, Measurement and Data, Geometry, and Mathematical Practices. Again, parents who want to know what specific skills or learning goals were addressed during the marking period can find this information in the online curriculum document. This resource describes, for example, the particular Number and Operations—Base Ten standards students worked on during the second marking period of third grade.

Note that teachers also provide marks for Process Goals in Mathematics. This option is provided because teachers frequently find that students behave differently during instruction in different subject areas. By providing marks for these process elements in each subject area, teachers can point out these differences when they exist, even in self-contained classrooms where one teacher is responsible for instruction in most or all subjects.

The portion of a secondary report card illustrated in Figure 2.2 shows a format somewhat different from that of the elementary report card, primarily due to differences in the way instruction is organized at this level. In elementary classrooms, the same teacher teaches multiple subjects to a single group of students. Because all students in the class are at the same grade level and are working on the same or comparable learning standards, the report card for all students in the class will look the same. At the middle school and high school levels, however, students take different classes taught by different teachers. Therefore, secondary standards-based report cards tend to be organized by classes or courses and often are arranged in the order of students' schedules. As a result, every student's report card will look somewhat different. This example shows the results from the first three classes in this student's schedule: Algebra I, Biology I, and Physical Education. The grades and marks for the student's other classes would be printed on the next page of the report card.

Another difference in this example of a secondary standards-based report card is the provision of three sets of marks rather than two. The first two marks relate to Achievement Grades and Standard Marks for academic performance within the subject or course. The third set of marks is for Process Goals.

Figure 2.1 Example Elementary Standards-Based Report Card

		Standard Marks		Process Marks	
Student: _____		4	Exemplary	++	Consistently
		3	Proficient	+	Sometimes
Reporting Period:		2	Progressing	-	Rarely
☐ 1st		1	Struggling	N/A	Not Assessed
☐ 2nd		N/A	Not Assessed		
☐ 3rd		*Modified standard. See progress report.*			
☐ 4th					

Teacher	Language Arts				
[Photo]	**Standard Goals**			**Process Goals**	
	Reading			Preparation	
	Writing	°		Participation	
	Listening			Homework	
	Speaking			Cooperation	
	Language			Respect	

Description and Comments:

Teacher	Mathematics				
[Photo]	**Standard Goals**			**Process Goals**	
	Operations and Algebraic Thinking			Preparation	
	Number and Operations—Base Ten			Participation	
	Number and Operations—Fractions			Homework	
	Measurement and Data			Cooperation	
	Geometry			Respect	
	Mathematical Practices				

Description and Comments:

Figure 2.2   Example Secondary Standards-Based Report Card

Student: _____	Achievement Grades		Standard Marks		Process Marks	
	A	Excellent	4	Exemplary	++	Consistently
	B	Good	3	Proficient	+	Sometimes
Reporting Period:	C	Basic	2	Progressing	–	Rarely
☐ 1st	D	Below Basic	1	Struggling	N/A	Not Assessed
☐ 2nd	U	Unsatisfactory	N/A	Not Assessed		
☐ 3rd	* Based on modified standards.		* Modified standard. See Progress Report.			
☐ 4th						

Teacher	**Algebra I—Mathematics 200**		
	Achievement		**Process Goals**
	Seeing Structure in Expressions		Participation
	Arithmetic with Polynomials and Rational Functions		Cooperation
	Creating Equations		Homework
	Reasoning with Equations and Inequalities		Punctuality
	Mathematical Practices		

Description and Comments:

Teacher	**Biology I—Science 205**		
	Achievement		**Process Goals**
	Basis of Scientific Inquiry		Participation
	Physical, Chemical and Cellular Basis of Life		Cooperation
	Continuity of Life and the Changes of Organisms Over Time		Homework
	Unity and Diversity of Life		Punctuality
	Ecological Relationships Among Organisms		

Description and Comments:

Teacher	**Physical Education—Health 200**		
	Performance		**Process Goals**
	Demonstrates Competency in Motor Skills and Movement Patterns		Participation
	Demonstrates Understanding of Movement Concepts, Principles, Strategies, and Tactics		Cooperation
	Engages Regularly in Physical Activity		Homework
	Achieves and Maintains a Health-Enhancing Level of Physical Fitness		Punctuality
	Exhibits Responsible Personal and Social Behavior that Respects Self and Others		
	Values Physical Activity for Health, Enjoyment, Challenge, Self-expression, and/or Social Interaction		

Description and Comments:

The Achievement Grades represent a culminating, summary judgment of students' achievement during the marking period in each course. These grades depict five levels of performance:

A = Excellent

B = Good

C = Basic

D = Below Basic

U = Unsatisfactory

Included with the summary Achievement Grade are individual Standard Marks. These marks are numerals (4, 3, 2, 1, and N/A) that show the student's level of performance on specific standards or strands of standards within each course. As they can with the elementary standard strands, families can find more detailed information on the specific skills or learning goals addressed during the marking period within that strand in an online curriculum document. The Standard Marks include the same four levels related to students' proficiency that were used in the elementary report card: Exemplary, Proficient, Progressing, and Struggling. Teachers use a variety of strategies in combining sources of evidence to determine the Standard Marks and in combining Standard Marks to determine the Achievement Grade. Although no strong research evidence supports one particular strategy for combining such evidence or marks, we recommend teachers consider the guidelines outlined in the box below. Whatever strategy they use, however, teachers must always be able to defend the grade they assign as an accurate reflection of students' culminating achievement at the time of reporting, and they must have evidence to support their decisions.

Guidelines for Combining Standard Marks

1. *Divide all evidence* gathered on students into one of three exclusive categories based on product, process, and progress criteria.
2. Within the grade book, *divide all product evidence* into two categories: *practice/formative* and *evaluative/summative*.
3. *No zeros* may be entered in the evaluative/summative category unless a student actually gets every question on an assessment wrong.

(Continued)

4. When assigning an overall grade or mark to a course or subject area, *ensure that the grade reflects the stated purpose*: It should be an accurate, meaningful, and defensible summary of what a student has learned and is able to do at this point in time in reference to stated standards for student learning.

In determining what grade or mark is the most accurate and defensible, it is usually best to

a. avoid the practice of averaging,
b. give priority to the most recent evidence,
c. give priority to the most comprehensive evidence,
d. give priority to the evidence related to the most important learning goals or standards, and
e. have valid and reliable evidence from multiple sources to support your decision.

Similar to the elementary report card, the secondary report card includes specific Process Goals that teachers assess in each course during the marking period. These ratings also relate to the consistency with which the student meets each goal and include the three levels *Consistently*, *Sometimes*, and *Rarely*; and *Not Assessed*. Just four categories of Process Goals are considered: Participation, Cooperation, Homework, and Punctuality. Again, while other process elements could be considered, these are the ones believed most important by the educators who developed this form.

In addition, the developers of this form decided to focus on only the frequency of process goals like Participation, rather than its quality. Some might argue that it would be helpful to distinguish between students who speak every day in class but say nothing of substance, and those who rarely speak but when they do, offer comments reflecting clear insight and careful reasoning. While reporting on aspects of quality is certainly appropriate, gathering and accurately recording such evidence can be challenging and time consuming for the teacher.

Families who want information about the specific criteria used to assign these Process Marks can find them in an online reference guide. The rubric for the "Homework" mark, for example, might describe the criteria for its marks as follows:

Consistently: All homework assignments completed and turned in on time

Sometimes: Only a few missing or incomplete homework assignments

Rarely: Numerous missing or incomplete homework assignments

As was true of the mark for Participation, these indicators focus exclusively on homework completion and set aside issues related to correctness or quality. Developing accurate indicators of other process elements like "Cooperation" can be exceptionally challenging but must be done if such a goal is to be included on the report card.

Below the legend are sections for each course in the student's program, listed in the order of the student's class schedule. Like those in the elementary example, each section includes a photograph of the teacher. Next is the Achievement Grade for the marking period, followed by a breakdown of the reporting standards for the course. Beside the Achievement section are listed the Process Goals assessed during the marking period. Below that is a Descriptions and Comments section where teachers can clarify what the class worked on during the marking period and offer individualized comments about the learning progress of students. This is also where teachers may note of the unique strengths or specific difficulties of struggling learners.

Advantages of Multiple Grades or Marks

When first viewing these forms, some educators express concern that completing them will require a lot of extra work. But teachers using such forms say that they actually require *less work* than traditional reporting forms. They do not require teachers to collect any additional information, and they eliminate the final step of deciding how to combine those diverse forms of evidence. As a result, all of the arguments and debates that arise about how best to weight and integrate the different sources of evidence to determine a single grade for the subject area or course can be avoided.

The teachers who use multiple grades or marks further maintain that students take process goals such as class participation and homework more seriously when these are marked separately. No longer can poor performance in these elements be disguised in an overall course grade. These teachers also say that reporting on separate standards helps them provide more specific guidance to parents concerned with what they can do to improve their child's achievement grade, especially if their child is a struggling learner. By providing different marks for each reporting standard, teachers help families focus their efforts at home on the specific concepts or skills with which their child is having difficulty.

Occasionally teachers question the need for this level of specificity in assigning grades or marks to students' performance. On further reflection, however, most discover that they already gather this kind of evidence, even when they assign a single grade to students. In determining an overall grade, teachers must decide how much credit to give students for their performance on each subject or course standard, as well as how they did in completing homework assignments and participating in class discussions. The same is true when reporting separate marks for homework and class participation. Now, however, teachers must ensure that students understand the various performance levels so that they know what their marks signify and what can be done to improve.

Reporting separate grades or marks for various product, process, and progress criteria also makes grading much more meaningful. Employers and college admission persons like it, because it offers more detailed information on students' accomplishments. With all grades reported on the transcript, college admissions officers can distinguish between students who earned high achievement grades with relatively little involvement and those who earned equally high grades through diligence and hard work. The transcript thus becomes a more robust document that presents a better and more discerning portrait of students' learning experiences (Adelman, 1999). For struggling learners in particular, separate grades or marks for these different types of goals makes both the report card and transcript more meaningful and informative documents.

Secondary schools still have the information needed to compute grade point averages and class ranking, if such computations are important. Now, however, those averages and ranks are untainted by ill-defined aspects of process or progress. As such, they represent a more valid and accurate measure of achievement and performance. Furthermore, to the extent that classroom assessments of students' performance and state assessments are aligned, the relationship between achievement grades and accountability assessment results will likely be much stronger (Willingham, Pollack, & Lewis, 2002).

Why Focus on Standards?

Occasionally, parents express skepticism about basing grades on standards and the usefulness of a standards-based report card. They believe that a traditional letter grade or percentage grade for each subject area on the report card works just fine, and they see no reason to change. Even the parents of struggling learners sometimes favor traditional grades, because they understand letters and percentages, or at least believe that they do, because that is what they received when they were in school two or three decades ago.

When initiating these reforms, educators need to pay special attention to helping parents understand the problems associated with traditional letter grades as well as the unique benefits of moving to a standards-based system. In particular, they need to help parents of struggling learners understand that when teachers assign a single letter grade or percentage to students for each subject studied or each course, they combine elements of achievement, skill, attitude, behavior, and work habits into that one mark, making it a confusing amalgamation that is impossible to interpret. This is not to imply that students' responsibility, participation, punctuality, cooperation, and other work habits are unimportant. Clearly they are important, especially when reporting on the performance of struggling learners who may have behavioral goals built into their individual plans. Teachers at all levels generally recognize the value of offering all students and families specific feedback on the adequacy of performance in these areas. A standards-based report card allows teachers to do precisely that by reporting on these nonacademic elements *separately*. As a result, parents have a clearer and more detailed picture of their child's academic performance in school, along with information about other, important school-related activities and behaviors (see Guskey & Bailey, 2010).

Furthermore, a standards-based report card breaks down each subject area or course into specific learning goals. The standards within each subject area offer families a more thorough description of their child's academic performance. A single grade of C, for example, might mean a modest level of performance on each of five different learning goals, or excellent performance on three goals but dismal performance on two others. Without the breakdown that standards-based reporting offers, this difference would be obscured. Standards-based grading provides a more comprehensive picture of students' academic performance as well as other factors that might contribute to their performance. It thus facilitates collaboration between families and educators in their efforts to help students improve their performance, especially those who may be struggling.

A standards-based report card identifies the specific learning goals within the curriculum so that appropriate rigor can be ensured. It communicates more detailed information about student learning progress with regard to those goals in order to bring about higher levels of success. For struggling learners, such a breakdown is essential for identifying their specific academic strengths as well as areas where additional time and effort may be needed. These benefits serve to prepare all students well, no matter what type of learning environment they enter in subsequent grades or even after they leave school.

Defining the Purpose

Another vitally important issue that must be addressed by educators engaged in standards-based reforms is defining the purpose of their standards-based report card. Three questions are paramount in these discussions: (1) What information will be communicated in the report card? (2) Who is the primary audience for the information? and (3) What is the intended goal of that communication? or How should that information be used? Answering these three key questions makes other critical issues about the form and structure of the report card much easier to address and resolve.

What Information Will Be Communicated in the Report Card?

While other types of report cards and reporting devices often contain widely varied types of data, the information offered in a standards-based report card is quite specific. In particular, four types of information must be included:

1. The explicit standards or learning goals students are expected to attain.

2. Whether or not those standards have been "modified" for a struggling learner. (This will be our focus in the next chapter!)

3. Each individual student's level of performance or proficiency in meeting the specified standards.

4. The adequacy of that level of performance or proficiency at the time of reporting.

In other words, a standards-based report card should clearly communicate what we want students to learn and be able to do, whether or not modifications were involved, how well they are doing those things, and if that level of performance is in line with expectations for progress at this time in the school year.

The standards included on the report card should be specific enough to communicate the knowledge and skills we want students to gain, but not so detailed that they lose their meaning and usefulness when shared with parents and others. This means the *reporting standards* included on the report card must be relatively few in number, clearly stated, and expressed in language that parents and others can understand (see Guskey & Bailey, 2010). The same is true of online curriculum documents that accompany the report card and explain to families the specific concepts or skills addressed during the marking period. For example, under the "Foundational Skills" language arts standard in the elementary report card, few parents are likely to understand the meaning of a standard labeled "develop phonemic awareness." On the other hand, most parents would know what it means to "understand the relationship between letters and sounds."

In addition, a standards-based report card must identify every student's level of proficiency or achievement with regard to each standard or standard strand. That is, not only must the expectations for student learning be clear, but so too must be each student's level of performance in meeting those expectations. This usually requires identifying three or four explicit steps that describe students' progress toward mastery or proficiency on each standard, along with specific examples drawn from students' work that represent each step or level.

The last type of information that must be included in a standards-based report card, and the one most often neglected, is an honest appraisal of the adequacy of each student's level of performance at this time in the school year. Parents frequently criticize standards-based report cards because often they do not communicate the *adequacy* of students' performance. Parents and others want to know how well their child is doing, but they also want to know whether or not that level of performance is in line with the teacher's and school's expectations. If it is not, they want to know what they can to do to help so that minor learning difficulties can be remedied before they become major learning problems. This is especially true of parents of struggling learners.

Who Is the Primary Audience for That Information?

The second question considered in defining the purpose of the report card is the primary audience for the included information. Again, while the audience for other types of reporting devices tends to vary, the audience for a standards-based report card is likely to be (1) parents or other adults, such as guardians or relatives, and/or (2) the students themselves.

Elementary educators rarely debate this matter. For them, the primary audience is definitely parents, guardians, and other adults. Because of the nature of most elementary classrooms, teachers regularly communicate with their students about each individual's learning progress. They let students know when they are doing well and when additional work or effort may be needed. Report cards are designed to bring parents up to date and keep them abreast of their child's performance and learning progress in school.

When queried about the purpose of the report card, parents express similar consistency in their perspectives: they believe the report card is for them. Parents see report cards as their primary communication link with teachers and the school regarding their child's learning progress. Why else would they be asked to sign the report card to ensure that they received it?

Middle grade and secondary-level educators tend to be more divided. Many believe, like elementary educators, that the primary audience is parents. To these educators, report cards serve to inform parents and other adults about their children's academic performance. Other secondary educators argue, however, that older students should be taking increased responsibility for their own achievement and accomplishments in school (see Guskey & Anderman, 2008). For these educators, report cards serve to inform students about their teachers' formal judgments of how well they have met established learning goals and expectations.

In some cases educators decide that the primary audience is *both* parents and students. While completely appropriate, this heightens the communication challenge. Under these conditions, specific steps must be taken to ensure that both parents *and* students understand the information included in the report card and can use it to guide improvements when needed. Especially for struggling learners, the report card should communicate meaningful information that both students and their parents comprehend and find useful.

How Should That Information Be Used?

Finally, the report card should offer guidance regarding how to use the included information. In other words, the report card should communicate *with intent*. Obviously, the best use of that information will depend on the primary audience. The report card may, for example, provide parents and others with information about their children's academic strengths and specific learning difficulties so that successes can be celebrated and explicit steps taken to remedy any problems. For students, it might recognize their accomplishments and identify areas where additional study is needed. The key point is that rather than offering a culminating, final evaluation, the report card should be seen as part of a continuous and ongoing communication exchange between school and home. Above all, the report card should relate information that both facilitates and coordinates efforts to improve student learning.

Developing meaningful, honest, and equitable grading policies and practices will continue to challenge educators at all levels. The challenge remains all the more daunting, however, if we continue to use reporting forms that require teachers to combine many diverse sources of evidence into a single symbol. Standards-based reporting allows teachers to offer better and more precise descriptions of students' academic achievement and performance along with important information about other vital learning goals. It facilitates communication between general educators and special educators who must coordinate their efforts in providing high-quality learning experiences for struggling learners. To the extent that process elements related to such things as formative assessment results, homework, class participation, cooperation with classmates, responsibility, and the like are important, they too can be reported, but they must be kept separate. Doing so will clarify the meaning of grades or marks and greatly enhance their communicative value.

Summary

In this chapter we described how the focus on standards provides a foundation for meaningful change in all aspects of education. Making clear our expectations for student learning gives direction to reform efforts by centering attention on what is most vital. We also explained the importance of distinguishing product, process, and progress goals for student learning and outlined the many advantages of using multiple grades for all students, especially those who are struggling learners. Finally, we described why it is important to define the essential purpose of the report card and discussed the crucial issues that must be addressed in establishing that purpose. In the next chapter, we will use this foundation to build more meaningful standards-based grading procedures for struggling learners.

3

The Inclusive
Grading Model

Before schools can implement fair policies and practices for grading exceptional and struggling learners, they first must have in place a high-quality grading and reporting system for *all* students. As we discussed in Chapter 2, this system should separate "product" goals related to academic performance and achievement from indicators of "process" and "progress." In addition, the product goals should *identify clear standards* that address specific aspects of academic performance. Once this foundation is established, schools can more easily develop procedures for determining grades for struggling learners that are fair, accurate, and meaningful. In this chapter we will describe the five steps of an Inclusive Grading Model (Jung & Guskey, 2007, 2010a, 2010b; Jung, 2009) that can guide educators in this process.

Five-Step Inclusive Grading Model

Earlier we described how teachers typically receive little guidance on how they should grade struggling learners. As a result, most arrive at the end of the grading period asking questions such as, "How do I accurately measure what my students have learned and are able to do?" and "How do I fairly report that level of performance? The majority of teachers answer these questions by making informal grading adaptations. But as we discussed in Chapter 1, those adaptations seldom result in grades that are meaningful or fair.

Instead of asking "How should I measure . . . ?" at the end of the marking period, a far better approach is for teachers to ask, "What should I measure?" at the beginning of the marking period. In other words, teams of educators working collaboratively should decide up front what are the most appropriate standards to measure for each student. Once these standards have been identified, measuring students' performance in relation to those standards can be clear, consistent, and equitable. Furthermore, with questions about what to measure and how to measure resolved, the process of grading becomes a lot easier.

This approach provides the basis for our Inclusive Grading Model, shown in Figure 3.1. The model's five steps are as follows:

1. Determine if adaptations are needed for each grade-level standard.

2. For each adaptation, determine if an *accommodation* or a *modification* is needed.

3. Establish the appropriate expectation for each area requiring modification.

4. Apply appropriate and equitable grading practices to the appropriate standards.

5. Clearly communicate the meaning of the grades.

Step 1: Determine if Adaptations Are Needed for Each Grade-Level Standard

Most exceptional and struggling learners work on grade level for some skills and below grade level for others. Even within a single subject area, these students are likely to have areas of strength and other areas that need to be targeted for improvement. A student like Norah from our snapshots in Chapter 1, for example, may have reading comprehension skills that are above grade level and fluency skills that are significantly below. Because of these differences, it is important to determine specifically where adaptations are needed for individual students and where they are not.

The first step in grading struggling learners involves considering *each* reporting standard for the grade level and deciding whether or not an adaptation to the standard is required for the student. An adaptation is needed if the team decides it is unlikely that the student will be able to meet the standard during the current marking period or academic year without any changes or special support. The team that makes this determination typically consists of the general classroom teachers, school

Figure 3.1 Inclusive Grading Model

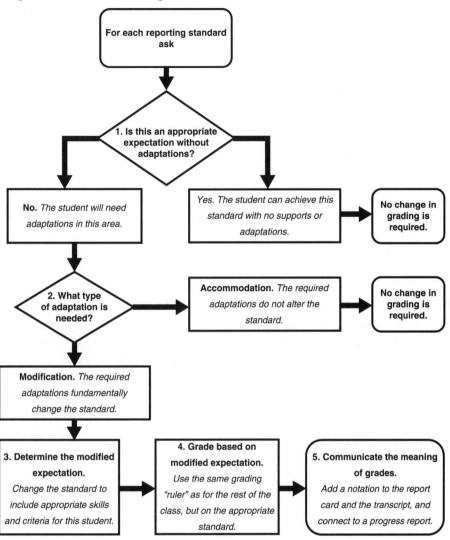

SOURCE: Jung & Guskey, 2010a.

administrators, parents, and any specialists who might be involved in the student's instructional program. In the case of Carlos, the fifth-grade English learner from our snapshots, this conversation may involve his two general classroom teachers, the school principal, his parents, and the EL teacher.

For Janis and Jimi in our snapshots, both of whom have disabilities, the entire individualized education program (IEP) team would engage in this conversation. Typically at the middle and high school levels, only one general education teacher participates in an IEP team meeting, even though students have many teachers. But in cases like

Janis's and Jimi's, involving *all* teachers in the conversation about adaptations is important, even if all are unable to attend every IEP meeting.

SNAPSHOT: Carlos

Carlos's team met and discussed each of the standards that students in fifth-grade language arts were expected to meet. Collaboratively, the team decided that almost all of the required standards needed to be adapted in order for Carlos to access the curriculum and make progress toward closing the gap with his peers. In general, most of the skills needed to be adapted to a lower grade level. The team noted, however, that Carlos's comprehension skills are very high when reading text in his native language. Although he has difficulty reading English text, when he is able to read it, or when it is read to him, he retains the information exceptionally well.

In this step of the Inclusive Grading Model, if a standard does not need adaptation for a particular student, there is no need to adapt the grading process for that standard. For standards that need no adaptation, teachers should *grade as they would any other student in the class*. The criteria expected struggling learners are expected to meet should be the same as those that all students are expected to meet. No penalty or advantage should be given because of the student's status as a struggling learner or for qualification for any special program. When adaptations are needed, however, the team should move to step 2 in the model.

Step 2: For Each Adaptation, Determine if an *Accommodation* or a *Modification* is Needed

Once teams identify standards that need adaptation, they must decide whether those adaptations are *accommodations* or *modifications*. Accommodations are adaptations that provide access to the general curriculum but *do not* fundamentally alter the grade level standards (Freedman, 2000, 2005).

SNAPSHOT: Janis

Janis has difficulty taking notes in her 10th-grade classes because of the learning disability that affects her abilities in written expression. Janis's IEP team determined that audiotapes of lectures in science and history are a very effective alternative for her. Because of her learning disability, Janis also may need to be administered assessments orally. Although the format for answering questions on assessments is different, the content of the questions and the substance of responses remain the same.

Providing Janis with an alternative mode of response does not lower the grade-level expectation. Having Janis take the assessment orally is an example of an accommodation.

SNAPSHOT: Carlos

Because Carlos is an English learner newly arrived to the United States, his teachers and family determined that social studies and science assessments need to be administered orally for a short time. They decided on this accommodation because his conversational skills are much stronger than his written academic skills in English. His teachers will measure the quality of his oral responses with the same criteria used to judge the performance of other students.

In the above example, Carlos's teachers are merely providing Carlos with access to the curriculum, not lowering the social studies standards. Therefore, in this case, taking the assessments orally is an example of an accommodation.

Some struggling learners, however, require more substantial supports in certain areas than accommodations can offer. For these students, some or all of the grade-level standards may not be achievable during the academic year, and curricular *modifications* are needed. A modification is an adaptation to the curriculum that fundamentally alters the grade-level expectation (Freedman, 2000, 2005). The instructional team decided, for example, that Carlos is unlikely to meet the grade-level standards in writing for language arts in fifth grade and modifications to most of the standards are needed. An IEP team similarly may determine that Jimi, the eighth grader from our snapshots who has Down syndrome, will not be able to achieve the eighth-grade mathematics standards this academic year. For Jimi, the mathematics standards will need to be modified in order to provide opportunities within mathematics that are appropriate for his present level of development. Although both types of adaptations are included in the IEP, historically teams may not have recorded accommodations and modifications differently.

Any of the four students from our examples could require *both* accommodations and modifications. Looking at Table 3.1 we can see that the team has decided that is exactly what Carlos needs—accommodations for some standards and modifications for others. Specifically, he needs modifications for most language arts standards, but only accommodations in the area of comprehension for both Reading (Key Ideas) and Writing. For grading and reporting purposes, making the distinction between accommodation and modifications is necessary for each reporting standard that requires adaptation. In Chapter 4 we discuss the distinction between accommodations and modifications in greater detail. After teams have determined which standards need to be modified, they can move to Step 3.

Step 3: Establish the Appropriate Expectation for Each Area Requiring Modification

For standards that need modification, the educational team has in effect agreed that the student is unlikely to meet that standard during the academic year. Assigning failing marks for grade level standards that the team has already determined inappropriate provides no helpful information about the student's performance or level of achievement. So instead, the educational team must establish modified expectations that student will be able to achieve with appropriate services or supports.

Modified expectations should be directly linked to the grade-level standards. Because most grade-level standards do not include prescribed criteria for evaluation, however, teams need to clarify specific expectations for that grade level. Then they must determine how those expectations can to be modified to give the struggling learner a reasonable chance at success.

Jimi, for example, may not be ready to work on eighth-grade science standards in mineral identification. The IEP team may choose to develop science standards on the skill of sorting and classifying that are fundamentally related to the eighth-grade science standards but are also developmentally appropriate for Jimi. For students with formal individualized plans, such as an English learner (EL) plan or an IEP, the modified expectation should be recorded as an annual goal with short-term objectives.

For Carlos, the team determines that two of the language arts standards require accommodations and all others need to be modified. Table 3.2 includes examples of modified curricular standards used in determining the grade for Carlos for the Language reporting standard. The curricular standards requiring adaptation are in the

Table 3.1   Accommodations and Modifications for Carlos

Language Arts		Type of Adaptation Needed	
Reporting Standards	**Curriculum Standards**	**Accommodation**	**Modification**
Reading	*Foundational Skills*		√
	Key Ideas and Details	√	
	Craft and Structure		√
	Integration of Knowledge and Ideas		√
	Range of Reading and Level of Text Complexity		√
Writing	*Text Types and Purposes*		√
	Production and Distribution of Writing		√
	Research to Build and Present Knowledge		√
	Range of Writing		√
Listening	*Comprehension and Collaboration*	√	
Speaking	*Presentation of Knowledge and Ideas*		√
Language	*Conventions of Standard English*		√
	Knowledge of Language		√
	Vocabulary Acquisition and Use		√

middle column, and the modifications deemed appropriate are in the right column. Notice that the reporting standards in the left column do not include specific criteria for evaluation. The team would have to discuss what is expected for fifth graders in language arts and what an appropriate expectation is for Carlos this academic year. The team has agreed that Carlos has skills on these standards at approximately the second-grade level and that he should be able to increase his skills to a fourth-grade level this academic year.

Table 3.2   Example Language Modifications for Carlos

	Grade-Level Curricular Standards	Modified Expectation
Language	*Conventions of Standard English*	*In his writing, Carlos will write in complete sentences with appropriate capitalization and subject-verb agreement in at least 80% of sentences.*
	Knowledge of Language	*Carlos will distinguish between and consistently use informal language for conversation and formal language in the academic setting.*
	Vocabulary Acquisition and Use	*Carlos will consistently distinguish between literal and figurative phrases (e.g., take steps) based on fourth-grade vocabulary in what he reads and writes.* *Carlos will demonstrate use of a fourth-grade vocabulary.*

For Conventions of Standard English, the team felt that a focus on complete sentences, subject-verb agreement, and appropriate capitalization was the appropriate target for Carlos in the upcoming year. In the area of Knowledge of Language, Carlos is having difficulty in distinguishing between the informal type of language that should be used when talking with his friends and the more formal language that is used in academic writing and speaking. His conversational skills are quite good, and he is ready to build his competencies in academic language. Similarly, although Carlos has a vocabulary of second-grade words, he does not yet have a mastery of nonliteral phrases (e.g., "I didn't catch that," "moving forward," "taking steps") that are often used in the English language. The team felt this was an important skill for him to make gains in this year.

Determining the modified standard is undoubtedly the most difficult step of the Inclusive Grading Model. For this reason we will expand on this step in Chapter 5. Once teams have determined the appropriate criteria for standards requiring modification, they can move to Step 4 in the model.

Step 4: Apply Appropriate and Equitable Grading Practices to the Appropriate Standards

Appropriately modifying the standards for a student answers the question, *"What* to measure?" The team determined that the grade-level standard was not appropriate and developed a modified expectation that represents the level of work the student is able to complete successfully. With questions about *what* to measure answered, adaptations to the grading process are no longer needed. Rather than basing the grade or mark on the grade-level standard, teachers can now assign report card grades *based on the modified expectation.*

Using this model, modifications are not based on students or subject areas, but on the individual reporting standards. In other words, it is not the *student* who needs to be modified for the standard, but certain *standards* that need to be modified for the student. For the majority of struggling learners, most grades will be based on grade-level standards. In subject areas where only accommodations are needed, struggling learners' grades should be based on the same criteria used to evaluate the performance of other students in the class with no penalty for accommodation. Carlos, for example, should be graded based on the content of his responses on his social studies assessments. The grade should not be lowered because he responded orally. It also should not be raised based on his attitude, effort, progress, or any other factor that is not a part of every other student's product or achievement grade.

For subject areas in which modified standards are used, grades should be based on the modified expectations, not the grade-level standard. Jimi, for example, is working on a modified expectation that involves sorting and classifying objects by simple characteristics rather than the grade-level expectation of mineral identification. There is no need to report a failing grade in science based on his inability to identify minerals. Nor would it be fair or meaningful to raise his grade because of his effort or behavior. Instead, Jimi should be graded on the standard the team determined was appropriate (e.g., Jimi will sort objects by size, shape, and color with 80% accuracy). Whatever grading scale is used for his classmates should be used for Jimi. On his report card, a 4 means exemplary, a 3 means proficient, a 2 means progressing, and 1 means struggling. Therefore, if he demonstrated exemplary performance and exceeded his goal, then he has earned a grade of 4. If he simply met his goal and demonstrated proficient performance, then he has earned a 3.

Similar decisions can be made for Carlos, who is working to build fourth-grade vocabulary in a fifth-grade class. Measuring and reporting progress on a standard the team has already agreed to be unattainable would be meaningless and, arguably, illegal. Adding points for homework or promptness in turning in assignments also does not make the product grade fairer. In fact, it distorts the grade's meaning. Instead, Carlos should be graded using the same "ruler," but on the fourth-grade vocabulary standards that the team deemed appropriate.

For Carlos, the team decided that his vocabulary goals should be to understand and use a fourth-grade vocabulary in general, and in particular to be able to understand the nuances of literal and nonliteral phrases and words with that vocabulary. Those are the skills on which his grade on the Vocabulary Acquisition and Use standard in language arts should be based. Table 3.3 includes an example of the progression from gradebook marks to overall grades for Carlos. Additional detail on monitoring progress for modified expectations is presented in Chapter 5.

Step 5: Clearly Communicate the Meaning of the Grades

Finally, teachers must provide additional information for the grades that are based on modified standards so that everyone is aware of exactly what was measured. Providing grades based on modified standards without communicating precisely what was measured is no more meaningful or fair than giving failing grades based on grade-level standards.

It is important to remember that some special notation, such as a superscript number or an asterisk, should be included on the report card and permanent record (or transcript) beside *each* grade that is based on modified standards. This notation for the standards the team agreed to modify can be seen on Carlos's report card in Figure 3.2 and Jimi's in Figure 3.3. An accompanying footnote might be worded, "Grade based on modified expectations," and direct the family to information about the standards on which the grade or mark was based.

By law, any notation on the transcript cannot identify the student as qualifying for special education services. Wording such as "special education goals" and "IEP goals," for example, cannot be used in transcripts, because these phrases identify the student as receiving special services. The wording "modified standard" is a legal notation, however, so long as modifications are available to any student, such as ELs and those receiving intensive intervention.

Report cards are different. Because the report card is considered a private document, designed only for parents and students, disclosing special education status in this context in not illegal. Nevertheless, broader notations on the report card, such as "based on modified standard," are preferable, since they can then be used for students who need modifications for a variety of reasons.

Table 3.3   Gradebook Marks and Overall Grades for Carlos

LANGUAGE ARTS: Reporting Period Two

Reporting Standards	Curriculum Standards	Assessment Marks									Summary	Grade
Reading	Foundational Skills*	2	2	3	2	3	4	4	4	4	4	
	Key Ideas and Details	3	2	3	3	3	4	4	4		4	3*
	Craft and Structure*	2	2	3	2	3	3	3			3	
	Integration of Knowledge and Ideas*	2	2	3	2	2	3	3	3	3	3	
	Range of Reading and Level of Text Complexity*	1	1	1	1	1	2	2	2		2	
Writing	Text Types and Purposes*	1	2	1	2	2	3	2	3	3	3	
	Production and Distribution of Writing*	1	2	1	2	3	3	3			3	3*
	Research to Build and Present Knowledge*	1	2	1	2	3	3				3	
	Range of Writing*	1	1	2	1	2	2	2	3	3	3	
Listening	Comprehension and Collaboration	3	3	3	4	3	4	4			4	4
Speaking	Presentation of Knowledge and Ideas*	3	3	4	3	3	4	4			4	4*
Language	Conventions of Standard English*	1	1	2	1	2	2	3	3		3	
	Knowledge of Language*	2	3	2	2	3	3	4	4	4	4	4*
	Vocabulary Acquisition and Use*	2	3	3	3	4	4	4			4	

*Grade based on modified expectations.

47

Furthermore, status as a student with a disability or EL is not information needed to understand progress. Families of students who have significant disabilities do not need another document that announces their child has a disability. They know that already. What matters for them and for the families of all struggling learners is that everyone understands what standard was measured and how the student performed relative to what was measured.

Figure 3.2   Example Language Arts Portion of a Report Card for Carlos

Elementary Report Card				
	Standard Marks		**Process Marks**	
Student: Carlos	4	Exemplary	++	Consistently
	3	Proficient	+	Sometimes
Reporting Period:	2	Progressing	-	Rarely
☐ 1st	1	Struggling	N/A	Not Assessed
☒ 2nd	N/A	Not Assessed		
☐ 3rd	*Based on modified expectations.*			
☐ 4th				

Teacher	**Language Arts**			
[Photo]	**Standard Goals**		**Process Goals**	
	Reading	3*	Preparation	++
	Writing	3*	Participation	++
	Listening	4	Homework	++
	Speaking	4	Cooperation	++
	Language	4*	Respect	++

Description: During this reporting period, the class spent time developing a multimedia news article based on a current event. Students are working on using formal fifth-grade vocabulary and rich descriptors in their writing and speaking. I want their news articles to have a logical flow with a beginning paragraph, several detail paragraphs, and a concluding paragraph. They will be working on these as they gain skills in new media and weaving these together creatively yet logically in the next two weeks.

Comments: Carlos has made remarkable progress in his gaining of third- and fourth-grade vocabulary, surpassing his goals. He has not yet mastered the fourth-grade level but is quickly progressing. His fluency is improving and is at about 40 words per minute with the grading passages he is given. He tries hard, and his exceptional comprehension shows his effort as well as his potential. I feel that with all he has learned this grading period, he is on track to meet his goals by the end of the year. With additional time spent in homework activities (he has missed a few), I think we can boost progress even quicker. Keep up the great work!

Figure 3.3 Example Language Arts and Physical Education Sections of a Report Card for Jimi

Secondary Report Card							
Student: Jimi **Reporting Period:** ☒ 1st ☐ 2nd ☐ 3rd ☐ 4th		**Achievement Grades**		**Standard Marks**		**Process Marks**	
		A	Excellent	4	Exemplary	++	Consistently
		B	Good	3	Proficient	+	Sometimes
		C	Basic	2	Progressing	-	Rarely
		D	Below Basic	1	Struggling	N/A	Not Assessed
		U	Unsatisfactory	N/A	Not Assessed		
		* Based on modified expectations.		* Based on modified expectations.			

Teacher	Language Arts		
	Achievement	**B***	**Process Goals**
	Reading Literature	3*	Participation ++
	Reading Informational Text	3*	Homework ++
	Writing	3*	Punctuality ++
	Speaking and Listening	3*	Effort ++
	Language	3*	
	Vocabulary	3*	

Description : This quarter our class focused on various forms of mass media communication and personal communication. Students analyzed news reports from different organizations and media outlets, comparing and contrasting forms and content. In personal communication, students wrote several types of business letters and reviewed aspects of formal conversation.

Comments: During this reporting period, Jimi continued to work on writing his name independently and has nearly mastered that skill. He has made wonderful progress in taking turns in conversation! He now uses active listening skills when another person is talking and contributes to the conversation when it is his turn. Keep up the great work!

Teacher	Physical Education—Health 200		
	Achievement	**A***	**Process Goals**
	Engages Regularly in Physical Activity	4	Participation ++
	Achieves and Maintains a Health-enhancing Level of Physical Fitness	4	Homework ++
	Demonstrates Competency in Motor Skills and Movement Patterns	4*	Punctuality ++
	Applies Movement Concepts, Principles, and Strategies	4*	Effort ++
	Respects Self and Others	4	
	Values Physical Activity	3	

Description: Our class learned about field sports this reporting period, particularly soccer, lacrosse, and field hockey. Students learned the rules of play in each sport, analyzed different field strategies, and had extended opportunities to play each.

Comments: Jimi really seemed to enjoy physical education this reporting period. He shows excellent sportsmanship and is always courteous and supportive of others. He has made fantastic progress this year in his motivation to be involved in exercise and sports. He has made remarkable improvement in his coordination as well.

Using the Inclusive Grading Model, anyone viewing the report card can see (1) how the student performed on the level of work that was appropriately challenging, and (2) which grades are based on work that is different from that expected at the student's assigned grade level. With this information, families and instructional teams can plan more effective intervention and make more appropriate placement decisions for students who are struggling.

Summary

In this chapter we described a five-step Inclusive Grading Model for assigning fair and meaningful grades or marks to struggling learners. The model focuses on the distinction between two types of adaptations to standards for struggling learners: accommodations and modifications. These adaptations are essential in standards-based grading. We showed how keeping this distinction in mind brings clarity to the reporting process and offers families more accurate information on precisely how their child is performing in school. Finally, we illustrated how modifications can be noted on report cards and transcripts. In the next chapter we will elaborate on Step 2 of the Inclusive Grading Model and offer additional information to help teams clarify the differences between accommodations and modifications.

4

Accommodations and Modifications

*The difference between the right word and the almost right word
is really a large matter—it's the difference between the lightning
bug and the lightning.*

—Mark Twain (1888)

In the second step of the Inclusive Grading Model presented in Chapter 3, we emphasized the importance of distinguishing between *accommodations* and *modifications*. This is an essential distinction in the model, because accommodations do not affect what is being measured and reported, but modifications do. Nevertheless, recognizing the differences between these two types of adaptation is not always easy. In fact, it is a distinction that can sometimes confuse general educators and special educators alike. So in this chapter we revisit the differences between these two types of adaptation and clarify their defining characteristics with regard to specific standards and individual students.

Definitions

Accommodations

In basic terms, accommodations simply allow students to participate fully in the instructional program. They can be thought of as similar to eyeglasses. A student who needs eyeglasses in order to see well is permitted to wear those eyeglasses in the classroom at all times. The eyeglasses simply give the student access to the material. They do not make the material easier for that student than for anyone else in the classroom. Rather, they allow the students to participate as fully as students who have better vision. In essence, eyeglasses simply level the playing field (Freedman, 2005) for that student. Accommodations serve in exactly the same way. Accommodations are supports that provide access to the general curriculum but do not fundamentally alter the learning goal or grade level standard (Freedman, 2000, 2005).

Modifications

For some students, however, an accommodation is not enough. These students need additional support in certain areas in order to be successful. In considering the educational background and learning history of these students, the educational team might decide that some or all of the grade-level standards are not achievable during the academic year, and some change or "modification" in the standards is needed. Unlike accommodations that simply level the playing field, modifications actually change the game (Freedman, 2005). Modifications are changes to the curriculum and assessments that do fundamentally alter the learning goal or grade-level expectation (Freedman, 2000, 2005).

Determining the Function of the Adaptation

From the definitions above, it would seem that we could construct a list of possible adaptations and then categorize each as an accommodation or a modification. Many schools, as well as numerous textbooks, websites, and articles, do exactly this. These lists of possible adaptations almost always consider "extended time" and "oral test taking" to be accommodations. But what many educators do not recognize is that these popular adaptations may or *may not* be accommodations. Subtle differences in context matter. Because of these contextual differences, few adaptations can be labeled as always an accommodation or always a modification. These contextual differences also must be noted in individualized education program (IEP) meetings and in the development of programs and corresponding forms.

Classifying a particular adaptation as an accommodation or a modification requires consideration of the circumstances of its use. Recall, accommodations do not fundamentally alter the grade-level expectation, but modifications do. Depending on the circumstances, therefore, an accommodation for a student in one subject area might actually be a modification for that student in another subject area.

Janis and Carlos, for example, are both permitted to respond orally on assessments. That adaptation would be considered an accommodation on assessments in science, so long as the science assessment is not measuring writing skills. If part of what is being measured includes writing skills, however, then responding orally fundamentally changes the standard or goal. In this case, the adaptation of responding orally would be considered a modification. So while being permitted to respond orally on most assessments in science or social studies might be considered an accommodation for Janis and Carlos, in language arts assessments designed to measure writing skills, it would be considered a modification. In the next section we explore examples of common adaptations and various circumstances in which each might be considered an accommodation or a modification.

Common Adaptations

1. Extended Time

One of the most common adaptations is extended time on an assessment or to complete an assignment. If the purpose of the assessment is to measure students' knowledge and understanding of particular concepts and not to measure speed or response rate, then extended time is an *accommodation*. And, indeed, the purpose of most assessments and assignments is to determine students' mastery of content or to provide evidence of a learning process, not to measure students' speed or rate of performance.

There are, however, instances when extended time is clearly a modification. One of those instances is if the assessment is specifically designed to measure students' speed or rate of performance. In certain math or reading assignments, such as "Mad Minutes" in mathematics and timed reading, for example, the provision of extra time would be considered a *modification*, because both accuracy *and* rate of performance are being measured.

SNAPSHOT: Norah

Because of Norah's difficulty with reading fluency, tasks that require reading are more time consuming for her. Her teachers are concerned that although she needs to continue working on her reading fluency, without adaptations she could fall behind in other subject areas. She is able to write her responses, too, but it always takes her longer. For this reason, Norah is given the adaptation of extended time on many school tasks and assessments.

For *most tasks*, giving Norah additional time does not make it easier for her than her classmates. Rather, having the extra time simply offers her the same access to the material as her peers. In language arts, however, extended time on assessments of reading fluency is a modification. This lowers the expectation on the fluency standard.

2. Complete a Task Orally

Allowing a student to take quizzes or exams orally is also a common adaptation for struggling learners. This adaptation is a great choice for students whose verbal skills are much higher than their writing skills, a scenario common to English learners and students with learning disabilities. Taking an assessment orally is an *accommodation* for any assessment that is not designed to measure proficiency in writing. If the assessment is connected to a grade or mark on a writing standard, however, it is a *modification*.

SNAPSHOT: Carlos

Carlos's fifth-grade teacher and English learner (EL) teacher met to discuss how he will participate in science and social studies assessments. He enjoys these subjects, but he has difficulty with his writing skills in both. His teachers determined that he needs to be able to take his social studies and science quizzes orally. Because he is learning English, and his conversational skills are much better than his written academic English skills, taking these quizzes orally will allow him to show more of what he has mastered.

For Carlos, taking quizzes orally in history or science is an accommodation. The adaptation does not make the content easier or in any way lower the expectation. This change merely allows him to express his knowledge and understanding in a different way. The quality of his responses also would be evaluated using the same criteria as are used for other students in the class.

3. Use Computerized Spell, Grammar, and Punctuation Check

For students who struggle with the conventions of spelling, grammar, and punctuation in writing, computerized word processors can serve as an excellent accommodation. As they work to complete written assignments, these students can concentrate on demonstrating fully what they have learned and are able to do, knowing that a prompt will be given for many of the spelling, grammar, and punctuation errors they might have. This use of computerized spelling, grammar, and punctuation checks is an *accommodation* for any assessment or assignment not connected to a grade or mark in conventions of writing. In subjects such as mathematics, science, or social studies, for example, the assessments are generally designed to measure students' understanding of concepts in those subjects, not their writing ability. To use word processing software to complete assignments in such subjects is an accommodation. On the other hand, this same adaptation would be considered a *modification* if the assessment or assignment focuses on a language arts standard and is designed to measure students' proficiency in the conventions of writing.

SNAPSHOT: Janis

Because of her learning disability, Janis experiences difficulties with the conventions of writing. Punctuation and capitalization are especially difficult for her. When given a prompt that there is an error, Janis is usually able to identify the error and correct it. But while she is writing, using the capitalization and punctuation skills that are automatic for most students in early elementary grades are tasks that require much concentration for her. Janis's IEP team determined that using a laptop computer and word processing program to complete her in-class assignments would be an appropriate accommodation for her. She is allowed to use this accommodation in all non–language arts classes. In language arts class, however, Janis and her parents decided that she will try to master this skill this year and will not use the adaptation in language arts class. The rest of the IEP team agreed that with practice and support in learning to identify errors in and revise her work, Janis is ready to work toward the grade-level expectation. If she had used the word processing program in language arts, it would have been a modification.

---

4. Complete Only Certain Parts of the Task

Reducing the length of assessments or assignments is an adaptation frequently chosen for struggling learners and for those who require additional time to complete tasks. This adaptation may mean fewer questions, problems, or tasks. And as is true of most adaptations, this can function as either an accommodation or a modification.

If all parts of the assignment address the same standard(s), and the length of the assignment is designed to provide more practice, then eliminating portions of the assignment is an accommodation. For example, a teacher might adapt an assignment of 100 two-digit multiplication problems by requiring that a struggling learner complete only 50. This adaptation is considered an *accommodation* as long as all 100 problems are of comparable difficulty. Instead of extending the time allowed, the redundancy in the task is eliminated.

Reducing the length of an assessment or assignment becomes a *modification*, however, when more difficult parts of the assessment or assignment are not required. A mathematics teacher, for example, may adapt an assignment by requiring that a student complete all of the two-digit multiplication problems but none of the three-digit ones. Because the more difficult items have been taken away from the task, the assignment has been modified.

SNAPSHOT: Norah

During social studies, Norah's second-grade class learns about each of the states in the United States by doing research online and using encyclopedias. Students are given 12 to 15 questions about each state and record their answers in a journal. Norah's general education teacher and reading specialists met to discuss how best to support Norah in this activity. They agreed that Norah has the skills to complete the task, but it will take her about twice as much time as it does her peers. At first, her teachers thought that having Norah research fewer states would be an appropriate accommodation. But, wanting to ensure that Norah felt as though she completed the project, they reconsidered. They discussed allowing her extended time to complete the task, but decided that would require too much of her time to be spent on this single task. Finally, the teachers agreed that the appropriate adaptation was to reduce the length of the assignment by requiring her to answer only 6 to 8 questions about each state. Because the purpose of the assignment is to increase library, encyclopedia, and research skills, Norah could demonstrate the same skills as her peers even though the length of the assignment was reduced.

Because Norah was expected to demonstrate mastery of grade-level skills, the adaptation of requiring fewer questions was an *accommodation*.

5. Take-Home Task Instead of In-Class Task

Having students complete a task in class can be the perfect way for a teacher to quickly check students' understanding of a concept and then offer immediate feedback. But for some struggling learners, the time constraints of the class period or the pressure of completing the assignment in the same way or at the same speed as others in the class is difficult to manage. In these circumstances, an educational team may decide to allow the student to complete certain assessments or assignments at home instead of in class. This adaptation is an *accommodation* if, and only if, all of the same relevant resources are available to the student at home as are available to students completing the assignment in class. On the other hand, if students taking a quiz in class, for example, are not able to use Internet resources, books, and class notes that are available to the student completing it at home, then this adaptation is a *modification*.

SNAPSHOT: Janis

Janis's eighth-grade teacher, her special education teacher, Janis, and her parents met to discuss her struggles in completing the increasingly difficult in-class papers being required in English Literature class. Janis said that because she was a slower writer, even when using her laptop, she felt self-conscious during the assignments. She did not feel she did her best work in class, because she was distracted by thoughts of how much longer her response took. Consequently, she had been submitting assignments before she had revised them and sometimes before she completed them. The team decided to allow her to complete some of her in-class, short paper assignments at home. By having Janis take home these in-class assessments and finalize them at home, she could devote more time and her full attention to the task.

The adaptation provided to Janis in the above example will provide her with greater opportunity to master the content. Because students in class are also able to use writing resources as they complete the short papers, Janis does not have any resources at home for this assignment that her classmates do not have. Thus, Janis's adaptation for this series of assignments is an accommodation.

6. Easier Tasks

When an educational team agrees that the grade-level expectation is inappropriate for a student, assignments and assessments can be changed to address expectations of a lower grade level. This may include adaptations such as reading text at a lower grade level, completing easier math problems, or mastering lower-level science skills.

Any time the grade-level expectation is lowered, the adaptation is a *modification*.

Students with more significant disabilities often work on a level of content that is multiple grade levels below that of their classmates. This may be true for only some subject areas or standards, but usually the level of work is different across most or all of the curriculum.

SNAPSHOT: Jimi

Jimi's IEP team met to determine his educational priorities for the upcoming year. Jimi is in 10th grade, and his special education and general education teachers collaborate to modify the curriculum to an appropriate level for him. Of the 36 standards on the report card, Jimi required modification on 32. His IEP team prioritized the standards and selected 8 to modify and include on the IEP as annual goals. For each of these 8 goals, Jimi is working toward elementary-level expectations. The changes in the standards do more than provide a different way to access or demonstrate content. The changes lower the expectation to a level that is attainable for Jimi. For example, a 10th-grade speaking/listening expectation is that students "respond thoughtfully to diverse perspectives, summarize points of agreement and disagreement, and, when warranted, qualify or justify their own views and understanding and make new connections in light of the evidence and reasoning presented" (CCSSO, 2010). Jimi's IEP team determined that a foundational skill that Jimi needs in order to work toward this standard is to "follow the standard rules of conversation, including (1) gaining attention from others in respectful ways, (2) actively listening to others using eye contact, and (3) taking turns to speak one person at a time."

The goals that Jimi's team developed are excellent examples of modifications that clearly connect to the general curriculum, despite the difference in expectation needed.

7. Changes to the Environment

Many struggling students need supports in the classroom environment to have access to an optimal learning experience. Students who are easily distracted, for example, may benefit from options such as completing assessments alone in a quieter area, sitting at the front of the classroom, or using a picture schedule. Adaptations to the environment like these are always *accommodations*. They do not alter the learning expectations; they merely are changes to the environment that make learning at the expected level more likely.

SNAPSHOT: Norah

Many second-grade students have some difficulty in dealing appropriately with distractions. Norah's teachers believe that because she is also struggling in the area of reading, though, that this normal distractibility is more of a concern for her. Consequently, her teachers decided she should sit at a table near the teacher's desk and with a group of students who do not frequently show distracting behaviors. By reducing distractions, Norah's teachers aim to create an environment in which mastery of reading is easier.

Examples of changes to the environment like those given to Norah in no way change the expectations for her learning. These are always accommodations.

8. Assistive Technology

Some students require the support of assistive technology. Assistive technology is any equipment or device made, adapted, or available commercially that provides access or improves functioning for a person who has a disability (Dyal, Carpenter, & Wright, 2009). Assistive technology includes equipment such as text readers, speech-to-text software, wheelchairs, and communication devices.

But assistive technology also includes devices, equipment, and software that are available to and used by the general public. The word processing software Janis used in the earlier example fits the definition of assistive technology, as does the video technology she uses in the example below. Widely available, commercial technologies such as these are considered "assistive technology" when they are used to improve access or functioning for a person with a disability. Any of these assistive technologies is almost always an *accommodation*.

SNAPSHOT: Janis

Janis's science teacher, special education teacher, and parents met to discuss how she might participate in the upcoming series of science projects. Each of these is a major assignment, and these assignments are repeated throughout the year. The science projects are connected to several of the standards each reporting period. Janis has difficulty in the area of written expression, and a significant portion of each science

(Continued)

project is a comprehensive paper that students write about their projects. Janis enjoys using technology and has shown an interest in video and web-based technology recently. Her teachers determine that she can complete the project by recording herself delivering a video presentation on all of the required components of the paper. In order to continue developing her writing skills, Janis will still complete the papers, and her special education teacher will give her feedback on these. But her science teacher will give her credit for mastering the content if she demonstrates it in *either* format. The teachers decided that allowing her to present her project through the video will provide her the opportunity to express what she knows about the content without the limitations her disability might otherwise impose.

Web-based and digital technology offer ever-increasing options for students to demonstrate mastery of content. By high school, almost all students have available to them computers with Internet connections, and many have mobile phones with video capabilities. Teachers and students can use these technologies in exciting, creative ways to adapt the curriculum for struggling learners. Because Janis's teachers are requiring her to demonstrate mastery of the same science content as her classmates, using video and web-based technology in this way is an accommodation that provides her access.

Summary

In this chapter we provided detail on distinguishing between accommodations and modifications. Most adaptations cannot be categorized as either an accommodation or a modification without understanding the context in which they are implemented. In fact, the same adaptation can be an accommodation for one standard and a modification for another. *Accommodations* are adaptations that provide students access to the general curriculum but *do not* fundamentally alter the grade-level standard. *Modifications*, on the other hand, fundamentally alter the grade-level expectation for students. Most struggling learners require accommodations for some standards and modifications to others. Adaptations should not be seen as pervasive or permanent. That is, a student may require adaptations for some subject areas and not for others, and as intervention is successful, the need for adaptations changes. In the next chapter we discuss an intervention planning and progress monitoring process that can be used to determine report cards grades based on modified expectations.

5

Measuring Progress on Modified Standards

With Gerry M. Swan

In the Inclusive Grading Model presented in Chapter 3, we introduced the idea of grading based on modified expectations. In this chapter, we provide an *intervention planning and progress monitoring* tool that can guide teams through determining the modified expectation and then grading on progress toward that expectation. The tool we describe works for struggling students who do not qualify for special services but also layers seamlessly over an existing English learner (EL), individualized education program (IEP), or Response to Intervention (RTI) structure.

In order to assign a grade based on a modified expectation, teams must have in place a systematic approach to monitoring progress toward individualized goals. Yet because most schools do not have a formal process in place, each team must select or develop a system for collecting data and monitoring progress. As educators navigate processes such as IEPs and RTI models, they are left with many questions. How should data be collected across subject areas and courses? Who on the team collects data? How should student progress be monitored and reported so that all stakeholders can interpret and use the information? How do educators determine if an intervention is successful?

Arriving at clear answers to these and similar questions about grading on modified expectations is extremely challenging. Remember, the federal special education requirement with which schools struggle the most is progress monitoring and reporting (Etscheidt, 2006). For students with disabilities, schools follow specific procedures for developing an IEP. During the IEP meeting, goals and services are selected for students. But even the IEP is not sufficient to guide daily progress monitoring and grading for exceptional learners. Instead, IEPs create the broad structure from which a more detailed and practical day-to-day plan can be developed.

Teachers face similar challenges with other struggling students (Bolt, Ysseldyke, & Patterson, 2010), ELs, and students receiving RTI. For these students, no standard structure like the IEP is available for intervention planning and progress monitoring. A variety of approaches have been recommended for implementing RTI models at the various grade levels and across subjects (Mellard, McKnight, & Woods, 2009). Because RTI's roots lie with early reading development, the resources for elementary general literacy outcomes are rich. In other subject areas and at the secondary level, however, there are far fewer places to which educators can turn for practical guidance (Fuchs, Fuchs, & Hollenbeck, 2007). Consequently, schools encounter tremendous variability in the way interventions are implemented and progress monitored (Bolt et al., 2010), as well as the way grades are assigned.

Certainly within any school there are many fine examples of data collection and progress monitoring for individualized outcomes. But there are advantages to having a progress monitoring form that is used consistently schoolwide. Most important, when data are collected and reported in a similar way across outcomes, everyone on the team, including parents and students, can more easily interpret progress information. Consistency across team members means that everyone needs to learn only one type of data sheet and one type of progress record.

From our snapshots in Chapter 1, for example, if Carlos's general education teacher and EL teacher both use the same type of progress record, Carlos's parents need to become acquainted with only one tool. Because Carlos's parents have limited experience with English, this is especially important. As a result, they will be able to focus on the progress instead of trying to understand many different types of data. When we effectively communicate information about the intervention and progress with families and students, they are able to participate more actively in making data-based decisions.

Critical Features of an Intervention Plan

The form in Figure 5.1 is based on the work of Baird (1994) and is designed to guide daily intervention and progress monitoring for individualized outcomes (see Jung, Baird, Gomez, & Galyon-Keramidas, 2008). Although the example form we have provided is only one of many solutions schools could choose, careful attention should be given to selecting a form. Merely changing the form can significantly impact the quality of plan that teams design for individual students (Jung, 2010). The critical features of the form include (1) measurable outcomes, (2) clearly defined intervention, (3) a data collection system, (4) visual data, and (5) a web-based platform.

1. Measurable Outcome

Once team members make the decision that a standard needs modification for a student, they face the task of selecting the appropriate modification and writing a measurable outcome by which to measure the student's success. This task is the most challenging step of the Inclusive Grading Model, primarily because most reporting standards do not include specific criteria. Therefore, to select the outcome for an individual student, the instructional team must first infer the criteria expected of students on grade level, and then determine the appropriate criteria for the student needing modification.

SNAPSHOT: Norah

For Norah, one reporting standard that needed modification was reading fluency. In the meeting with Norah's second-grade teacher and reading specialist, her general education teacher explained that students in second grade should be reading 90 words per minute by the end of the school year. Together, the two teachers determined that the appropriate expectation for Norah would be 60 words per minute.

Examples of modifications for Norah, Carlos, Janis, and Jimi are included in Table 5.1. For most students the connection between the grade-level expectation and their modified expectation is clear, with only a slight change in the criteria. This is the case for Janis, Norah, and Carlos. But for other students, like Jimi, the differences in criteria are far greater. Even when a student is working on objectives that are multiple grade levels behind that of his or her grade-level peers, however, the connection between the skills should still be apparent.

SNAPSHOT: Jimi

One expectation for eighth-grade mathematics students involves completing two-step algebraic operations. Distant but foundational skills for being able to complete this task are the ability to group like items and to add numbers up to 10. Because Jimi is not yet completing mathematics problems without using objects, his goal involves using a variety of manipulatives for counting and sorting. So far, he has learned to group and sort objects by one characteristic, and he can count using the objects. His goal, then, is to add numbers up to 10 using the objects.

Table 5.1 Modified Expectations Developed From Grade-Level Reporting Standards

Student	Grade-Level Reporting Standard	Grade-Level Expectation	Modified Expectation
Norah	Reading Fluency	Read 80 words per minute, smoothly, and with intonation.	Read 60 words per minute, without excessive errors.
Carlos	Writing	Convey information about a topic by introducing it clearly, grouping information logically, linking thoughts with transitioning words, and using appropriate formatting.	Using third-grade vocabulary, convey information about a topic, by introducing it and grouping information in paragraphs with correct sentence structure and punctuation.
Janis	Range of Reading	Read and comprehend 10th-grade literary nonfiction independently and proficiently.	Read and comprehend eighth-grade literary nonfiction proficiently with scaffolding.
Jimi	Operations and Algebraic Thinking	Complete two-step algebra problems.	Add and subtract numbers up to 10, using objects.

Two types of outcomes are included in the intervention plan: an annual goal and a short-term objective. In the example intervention plan (see Figure 5.1), the annual goal is in the top block of the form. Annual goals provide the target that guides intervention. For students who have disabilities, selecting annual goals occurs as a part of the IEP.

Annual goals need to have both *specific skills or behaviors* and *measurable criteria for success*. Students and members of the educational

Figure 5.1 Screen Shot of a Web-Based Intervention Plan

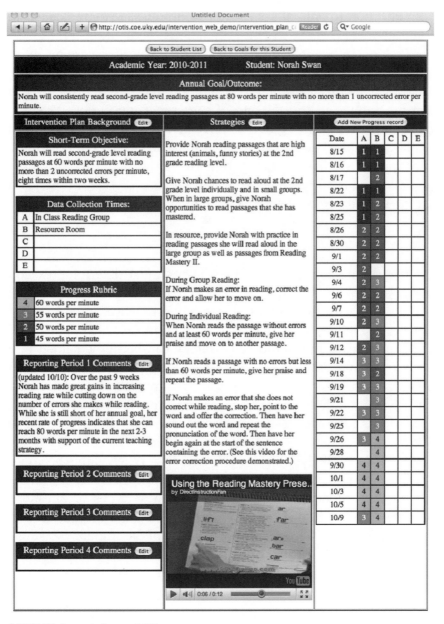

SOURCE: Jung & Swan, 2011.

team can then read the goal, know exactly what skill or behavior is expected, and know how progress is to be determined. A vague outcome, such as "reading will improve," is insufficient, because it could be interpreted so many different ways. It could mean "reading orally with fewer errors," "reading at a faster pace," or "reading by grouping phrases more fluently." On the other hand, Norah's annual goal from the intervention plan example tells us exactly what is expected: We expect her to "read second-grade level reading passages at 80 words per minute with no more than 1 uncorrected error per minute."

In addition to annual goals, short-term objectives are needed to serve as benchmarks in reaching the annual goal. Short-term objectives look much like the annual goal, except the criteria are meant to be achieved within 9 to 12 weeks. These 9- to 12-week objectives provide teachers with clear criteria for judging if a student is on track to meet the annual goal at the end of each reporting period. Progress monitoring is thus streamlined within existing report card periods. In Norah's example, her short-term goal is shown in the top box of the left column. If she has met her reading fluency objective by the end of the nine-week reporting period, it is clear to everyone on the team that she is on track to meet the annual goal.

2. Clearly Defined Intervention

Once the outcomes are defined, teams must determine exactly what strategies will be put into place to reach the outcomes. Federal legislation calls for the use of research-based practices in intervening with struggling learners (No Child Left Behind Act, 2008).

But any given research-based strategy can be implemented in a number of ways. To maximize the effect of any intervention, it must be implemented with *fidelity* (Kutash, Duchnowski, & Lynn, 2009). That is, interventions should be implemented the same way each time. Selecting the specific intervention approach requires teachers to address questions such as "What are the student's interests?" "When is this skill most likely to be demonstrated?" "When is this behavior a problem?" and "How does the intervention mesh with various parts of the curriculum?" Teams address these types of questions when they decide how an intervention should be individualized to best match the general curriculum *and* needs of the student. No single individual designs the final plan. Rather, it reflects the expertise and ideas of all team members, including families.

In the example for Norah, a direct instruction approach (Engelmann, 1999) is being taken. For her intervention plan, presented in Figure 5.1, the team provided additional details about how that approach will be used in both the general education classroom and the resource room. The procedures used in each setting were designed collaboratively and then documented in the plan. Recording the details of intervention in this way is a key to ensuring fidelity. Furthermore, knowing what intervention was implemented and exactly how allows us to say with greater certainty to what we can attribute progress (Kutash et al., 2009). Alternately, if there is insufficient progress, knowing the details of the intervention can help the team in revising the strategies.

3. Data Collection System

After outcomes are determined and intervention is planned, the team determines a data collection system for ongoing progress monitoring. Because data should drive decisions on intervention, progress monitoring is among the most critical components of successful intervention (Stecker, Fuchs, & Fuchs, 2008). Developing the data collection system involves decisions about (a) when progress data will be collected and (b) the rubric for scoring progress. The data collection times in the example intervention plan form are in the block along the right-hand side with column headings A–E in Figure 5.1. The rubric is numbered 1–4 and is in a block in the left-hand column beneath the data collection times.

Data Collection Times

A primary consideration for data collection times is the schedule of the classroom. For most objectives, times should be selected that fit naturally within the school day and blend well with the teacher's instructional schedule. Data collection times might be four different subject periods, such as science, history, math, and language arts. Selecting data collection times across subjects in this way may be useful when teams want to ensure a skill, such as writing, is demonstrated across the curriculum.

In Norah's example, progress data are to be gathered during large group reading in the general education classroom (A) and during her time in the resource room (B). Although there is space on the intervention plan form to collect data at five points, teams need to select only the number of times they feel are needed. In this example, the team selected two settings. Data do not have to be collected every day or in every selected setting/time. As the example shows, there are blank sections where data were not collected. And there were school days during which no data were collected at all. Nevertheless, sufficient data must be gathered to show clearly the increments of progress over time.

Progress Rubric

To collect data that can be easily translated to a grade, a progress rubric should be developed to quantify a student's progress. The progress rubric for the intervention plan should include the same number of levels as the report card. So, if a five-point grading scale is used on the report card, a five-point rubric should be used in the intervention plan. In the example report cards we described earlier, four levels of performance are used. Therefore, the intervention plans that correspond also include four levels of performance.

In the four-level progress rubric, Level 1 corresponds with the student's level of performance at the beginning of this intervention plan. Level 4 includes the criteria to meet the short-term objective (not the annual goal). Levels 2 and 3 are two intermediate points between Levels 1 and 4. Norah is reading at 45 words per minute, so, this becomes Level 1 on her plan. The nine-week objective is to be reading at 60 words per minute, which becomes the Level 4 criterion. The team chose two intermediate criteria between Levels 2 and 3. When translated to the report card, if Norah is reading 45 words per minute at the end of the reporting period, that is interpreted as struggling. Reading 60 words per minute would be considered exemplary.

Other objectives may not lend as intuitively to a rubric as rate of reading. Reading comprehension, for example, also will require the team to consider what should be measured and how.

SNAPSHOT: Janis

In Janis's IEP meeting, the team discussed her difficulty with reading comprehension. Her comprehension has improved recently, and she does well answering comprehension questions about eighth-grade reading material. But she is still unable to answer comprehension questions about *grade-level* reading material. Typically, she is unable to answer correctly more than one of five comprehension questions about a 10th-grade reading passage. The team determined that the appropriate objective would be, "After reading a 200- to 300-word 10th-grade reading passage, Janis will correctly answer five comprehension questions about the story." The rubric for this objective is in Table 5.2.

In order to write measurable outcomes, instructional teams need to be familiar with the multiple ways to measure progress. Too often teams become stuck in a pattern of using the same or similar criteria for every outcome. An example of a commonly used criterion is "with 80% accuracy." For many standards, however, accuracy is not the best

Table 5.2 Comprehension Progress Rubric

Rubric	
4 =	5 of 5 questions correct
3 =	4 of 5 questions correct
2 =	3 of 5 questions correct
1 =	2 or fewer questions correct

way to measure. For certain standards, accuracy may not even be a possible way to measure!

Consider Carlos's need to work on academic vocabulary as an example. The team may decide that he needs to master the high-frequency words for fifth grade. A goal to "read the Dolch sight words for fifth grade with 80% accuracy" would make little sense. There is no way to measure how accurately a student reads a word. For sight words, the important criterion is how quickly each word is recognized and read. A better wording, then, is "Carlos will read each of the Dolch sight words within two seconds of being presented with it."

4. Visual Representation of Data

Teachers and families need detailed information on students' progress that they can easily understand and interpret. Charts and graphs serve this purpose well (Schmid, 1954). Visual representation allows educators to share information with all families, including those who have limited literacy skills or different native language.

Historically, line graphs have been used to visually represent progress data. An alternate method of visual representation is simply to color code the data collection sheet. In Figure 5.1, the data are shaded in gray scale. Although in gray scale the progression from the darker ratings (1s) to the lighter ones (4s) is clear, the actual web-based application uses red, orange, yellow, and green to create a more pronounced visual effect. By using a color-coding method, the progress record is visual and easily illustrates Norah's progress toward her objective. The separate columns for each data collection time allow teams to see in which settings Norah made the quickest progress. At the end of each reporting period, a narrative explanation is added and a printed copy of the intervention plan is given to families as the progress record.

5. Web-Based Platform

Each of the first four critical features of the intervention plan contributes to the integrity of the intervention. The fifth critical feature ensures that the intervention planning process is practical and can be used to scale. Although the intervention plan provides a useful structure for managing progress data, technology is necessary for full, team-based implementation. In our earlier work, we found that when teams were trained to use the intervention plan on paper, collaboration in intervention design and data gathering were rare. This is partly because a paper form can exist only in one physical location. Much like a wiki, the online format allows for multiple team members to access and contribute to the most current version of the plan without any extra coordination efforts.

The web-based format also improves the efficiency of visually representing progress. As Figure 5.2 shows, any team member can click on a button to add a progress record, enter the date, and record the data point. Data are automatically color coded and added to the display. This makes information on progress available in real time to everyone on the team. Furthermore, because the data are part of a larger database, schools can visually examine trends in the data over time by student, classroom, or team member.

Our work with schools indicates that teams find the web-based intervention plan easy to use and manage and extremely valuable. Others have found that students in classrooms using technology-based

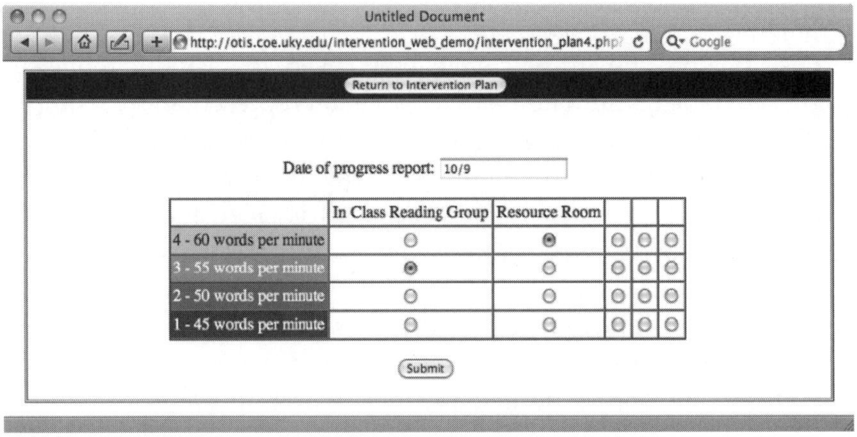

Figure 5.2   Screen Shot of Prompt for Adding a Progress Record

progress monitoring outperformed those in classrooms without this technology (Spicuzza, et al., 2001; Ysseldyke, Spicuzza, Kosciolek, and Boys, 2003). Seemingly, better and more efficient tools for progress monitoring lead to better instructional decision making and improved student outcomes.

In addition to improving the utility of the intervention plan, the online format also opens exciting opportunities for including multimedia resources. In Norah's plan, for example, a short video is added so that anyone on the team can watch and see the intervention in action. This can be especially useful when the intervention is implemented by more than one person across settings. The video for Norah's example was taken from a public-use website. But it could include a team member explaining an intervention or a short video of the student engaged in intervention activities. Other types of media could be included as well. A physical or occupational therapist, for example, could include photos of a positioning or support strategy. Any of these multimedia resources provides an additional resource to ensure fidelity of the intervention.

Pulling It Together for the Report Card

Once the Inclusive Grading Model is implemented, assigning a grade is a relatively simple process. At the end of the reporting period, teams can easily and quickly evaluate the effectiveness of the intervention by examining the visual progress record and any notes taken. In Step 5 of the Inclusive Grading Model, we suggested the need to make clear on the report card which grades were based on modified standards. If a grade on the report card is based on a modified standard, a symbol should be recorded beside the grade to indicate that.

SNAPSHOT: Carlos

For Carlos, the report card grades for standards in Writing were based on modified expectations. Recall from Chapter 3 that the expectations for all of the curricular standards that make up the grade for Writing were modified. He met the modified expectations for each of these skills (Text Type and Purposes, Production and Distribution of Writing, Research to Build Present Knowledge, and Range of Writing at the level of 3, or proficient. Therefore, on his report card in Figure 5.3, a 3* appears as the grade for Writing.

Figure 5.3   Example Language Arts Report Card Section for Carlos

Elementary Report Card					
		Standard Marks		**Process Marks**	
Student: Carlos		4	Exemplary	++	Consistently
		3	Proficient	+	Sometimes
Reporting Period:		2	Progressing	-	Rarely
☐ 1ˢᵗ		1	Struggling	N/A	Not Assessed
☒ 2ⁿᵈ		N/A	Not Assessed		
☐ 3ʳᵈ		*Modified standard see progress report.*			
☐ 4ᵗʰ					

Teacher	Language Arts				
[Photo]	**Standard Goals**			**Process Goals**	
	Reading		3*	*Preparation*	++
	Writing		3*	*Participation*	++
	Listening		4	*Homework*	++
	Speaking		4	*Cooperation*	++
	Language		4*	*Respect*	++

As with all standards-based grading, decisions about the grade are based on the student's mastery of the skill (Guskey & Bailey, 2010). Basing a grade on mastery means that the traditional way of summarizing performance by averaging scores is not appropriate. For struggling learners, the only purposes of the first three quarters of data points on the intervention plan are to (1) help paint the full landscape of progress for a student and (2) act as a formative assessment (Jung & Guskey, 2007) that guides how teams carry out intervention. These data points in the first three quarters of the reporting period *should not* be part of an average or even considered in determining the report card grade for modified standards.

Averaging Norah's performance on her reading objective, for example, would cause her to have a report card grade of 2*, which means progressing. But Norah mastered this objective! In standards-based grading on modified expectations, we must consider the *most recent, consistent* evidence of performance. In Norah's example from Figure 5.1, the reporting period ended on October 15. Her grade should clearly be a 4*, because the recent consistent evidence indicated that she had mastered the objective to that level. On the other hand, if most of her scores in the last two weeks of the reporting period had been 3, with only a few data points being rated 4, then a 3* would have been the more appropriate final grade.

At the end of each reporting period, narrative should be added to each intervention plan to summarize progress on the objective in response to the intervention used. This is the place to share information about strategies that seemed particularly effective or ineffective. The intervention plan narrative is also useful in providing additional information on a data point that is unusual or unexpected.

SNAPSHOT: Jimi

Jimi's teacher noticed that he was not performing as usual across several of his objectives during one week. On Wednesday, she learned that Jimi's medication dosage had been changed over the weekend, and the change was affecting his attention and alertness. The teacher then added narrative to the intervention plan on Wednesday explaining that Jimi had not been feeling well that week. At the end of the reporting period, Jimi's teacher reviewed his data as well as the narrative that had been added. In the two weeks before the end of the reporting period, Jimi's performance was consistently scored a 4 on most of his objectives, with exception of the three days after his medication change. The teacher, taking into account the medication change, assigned report card grades of 4 on these objectives. She also made a note of this in the narrative summary of his progress and the explanation of the outlier data points.

At the time report cards are completed and delivered, progress reports should be provided for any student receiving specially designed intervention. For students who are receiving special education, this progress report is a federal requirement (IDEIA, 2004). When teams use an intervention planning and progress monitoring form, there is no need to collect additional data and generate a separate progress report. Instead, with the addition of a summary narrative, the form *is* the progress report.

Summary

In this chapter we described an intervention planning and progress monitoring process that can be used with any exceptional or struggling learner. The form we presented includes five critical features: measurable outcomes, clearly defined intervention, a data collection system, visual representation of data, and a web-based platform. Once the intervention plan is implemented, determining a grade at the end of the reporting period is a relatively easy decision. Teachers simply review the visual progress record, focusing on the consistent evidence for the last two to three weeks of the reporting period in order to select a grade. By adding narrative that describes the student's progress, the intervention plan can then be shared with families as the progress report. In the next chapter, we address the steps that are needed for schools to implement the Inclusive Grading Model.

6

Facilitating Change

Our focus to this point has been on developing fair, accurate, and meaningful grading procedures for exceptional and struggling learners. We discussed the importance of separating product, process, and progress learning goals and offering separate marks for each. We described and gave examples of accommodations and modifications for struggling learners with different learning challenges. We also presented a five-step Inclusive Grading Model that organizes the decisions educators must make to ensure that grades are both honest representations of students' performance in school and legally defensible.

In this chapter we turn our attention to implementation and how to facilitate change. Putting these ideas into practice will require confronting some well-established and long-held traditions. As described earlier, some of these traditions are based on mistaken perceptions about what is fair or motivational for struggling learners. Others stem from predispositions based on individuals' personal experiences with grading. Regardless of the source, challenging these traditions takes knowledge of the research on what is truly best for struggling learners and a strong sense of commitment to putting that knowledge into practice. It also takes patience, perseverance, and courageous leadership at all levels.

We will consider facilitating change at three levels: (1) what teachers can do, (2) what administrators can do, and (3) what higher education institutions can do. Each of these levels has a unique and powerful influence on the change process that must be recognized and addressed. To a large extent, however, these levels also overlap: What happens at one level often influences the other levels. Furthermore, our experience indicates that failure to implement change at one level can impede and sometimes prevent change at other levels. Successful change efforts invariably involve comprehensive and coordinated actions at all three levels.

What Teachers Can Do

Of all levels of change, none is more important or more vital to success than the changes that teachers can make in their personal grading policies and practices. While many schools and school districts have established grading policies, these policies typically offer only broad guidelines for practice, often based on the format restrictions of their computerized grading program. Furthermore, these policies seldom discuss the unique challenges associated with grading struggling learners. As a result, individual teachers have great latitude in determining their classroom grading policies and practices, especially when it comes to assigning grades to struggling learners. Modest changes on the part of teachers, however, can have a powerful impact on the accuracy and meaningfulness of the grades they assign.

1. Implement Practices Guided by Knowledge Rather Than Tradition or Emotion

Too often the teachers' grading policies are based on what was done to them when they were students and on their personal beliefs fashioned by those experiences. Rarely are those policies based on established knowledge or research about effective practice in grading and reporting. This occurs because teachers' professional learning experiences hardly ever include in-depth discussions of that knowledge or research. No one talked about grading in their undergraduate education classes, their graduate classes, or in any of their professional development experiences. In addition, much of popular literature on grading is based on opinion and conjecture rather than research-based evidence on best practices, especially when considering struggling learners.

As we guide teachers in developing more effective grading policies and practices, we often begin by having them think back to their days as students and their personal experiences with grading. Specifically, we ask them to consider what they regard as their very best and absolute worst grading experiences. They then share those reflections with their colleagues, describing the nature of the experience and its influence on their perspectives about grading. The results of these discussions are always insightful, instructive, and strikingly consistent.

The nature of the worst grading experiences inevitable relates to issues of fairness and accuracy. We constantly hear statements such as "the teacher wasn't fair," "I got a low grade because the teacher didn't like me," or "the grade had nothing to do with what I learned or the quality of my work" (see Guskey, 2006a). These reflections offer powerful evidence about what must guide teachers in developing their own classroom grading policies and practices.

Above all other considerations, students should see a teacher's grading policies as fair and accurate. This means that such policies cannot be disguised or hidden from students. Instead, they must be explicit and transparent. Students should know the criteria on which their grades are based and the procedures used to determine their grades. They should understand the teacher's expectations for their learning and be able to determine how well their performance aligns with those expectations. If students are ever surprised by the grade they receive, something is amiss in the teacher's grading policies or procedures.

It also means that grading policies must be based on established research evidence of best practice (Guskey & Bailey, 2001; Guskey, 2009). What was done to many teachers when they were students was likely based more on tradition than on solid research evidence about what works best for students. Modern teachers must seek out that research evidence to ensure that their policies and procedures reflect the most current knowledge on effective practice.

Teachers must keep in mind, however, that such research evidence generally will not be found through a simple Google or Yahoo Internet search. Anyone with an opinion on grading can post it on the Internet, regardless of how well informed that opinion might be. Instead, teachers need to become familiar with using resources such as the Education Resources Information Center (ERIC) (www.eric.ed.gov/) system and other established research databases. These research repositories can offer the evidence teachers need to ensure that fairness and accuracy provide the basis of all grading policy decisions.

When we ask teachers to reflect on their best personal experiences with having their work or performance graded, we find similar consistency. Best experiences most often relate to an exceptionally challenging assignment that required lots of work, the teacher offered specific guidance for completing the task and detailed feedback along the way, and the grade was a fair and accurate assessment of what was accomplished (Guskey, 2006a). Again, this shows why the premises of fairness and accuracy must guide teachers in developing their own personal grading policies and practices.

2. Know the Difference Between Accommodations and Modifications

As we discussed earlier, the tables included in many publications that list certain adaptations as accommodations and others as modifications are never completely accurate. Whether a particular practice is considered an accommodation or a modification depends on the identified needs of the learner and the specific standard being addressed. The distinction that needs to be kept in mind is whether the practice simply allows the student to participate fully (i.e., levels the playing field) or fundamentally alters the nature of the standard (i.e., changes the game).

Although these are vitally important decisions, they are not decisions that teachers need make on their own in isolation from colleagues. Typically these decisions are made collaboratively by a team whose members are familiar with the student, know the details of his or her previous learning experiences, and understand the nature of the specific standards in question. Nevertheless, since teachers work most closely with students, their voices in these decisions often carry the most weight. For this reason teachers at all levels must be keenly aware of the crucial distinction between accommodations and modifications.

3. Think Big, but Start Small

There is no easier way to sabotage change efforts than to take on too much, too quickly. That is why implementing changes in grading policies and practices must be seen as a gradual process that may require several years. It is far better to begin small, making a few meaningful changes and implementing them well, than to attempt to incorporate an entirely new system of grading and reporting that provokes seemingly insurmountable challenges that then limit or preclude success.

One of the most meaningful and most important changes that teachers can make immediately for struggling learners is to separate product, process, and progress learning goals and to report on each area separately. This is easy to do, because it requires no additional work. Most teachers already record evidence on each of these areas separately. It is also the foundation of any form of standards-based grading. Grades become much clearer and far more significant when these different learning goals or standards are made explicit and separate grades or marks are provided for each.

Another important initial step is to develop better and clearer criteria for documenting students' levels of performance. All students, and especially struggling learners, benefit from feedback on their learning progress (Hattie & Timperley, 2007). But not all feedback is equally important. The best feedback is both diagnostic and prescriptive. In other words, it helps teachers and students identify precisely what was learned well and where additional work may be needed. It also offers guidance and direction for remedying identified learning difficulties. In order to be both diagnostic and prescriptive, feedback must be based on clear criteria related to students' levels of performance. Criteria that include examples of performance based on student work are particularly informative.

4. Initiate Frequent, High-Quality Communication With Families

Families of struggling learners often grow frustrated with the lack of information they receive from the school and especially from teachers about the learning progress of their children. This does not mean, however, that they want to receive report cards more frequently. Parents of struggling learners seldom find traditional report cards to be particularly informative or helpful. In fact, most describe the information included in the typical report card as vague, imprecise, and insufficiently prescriptive (Jung, 2009). What families want is specific, accurate, and meaningful information, offered on a regular basis in a form that they understand and can use.

To provide the families of struggling learners with this kind of information, teachers need to take advantage of a wider variety of communication tools (Guskey & Bailey, 2001). Monthly or twice-monthly progress reports can be useful, especially if they are part of established reporting routines. Regularly scheduled open-house meetings, parent–teacher conferences, and student-led conferences provide many valuable benefits (see Guskey & Bailey, 2001). Less formal means of communication can be effective as well. Personal letters or notes sent with the report card or, at other times, e-mail messages and phone calls, for example, are especially useful ways to communicate with the families of struggling learners.

When using these various forms of communication, it is best to begin on a positive note, perhaps describing the progress the student has made on specific academic tasks. Starting on a positive note sets parents' minds at ease and can open the conversation to a broad range of issues. It also helps parents and guardians see that the teacher is aware of the student's positive attributes. Asking about students' special interests and involvements outside of school during these conversations can help teachers develop more engaging lessons and involve struggling learners in more meaningful ways (Henderson & Berla, 1994; Hoover-Dempsey & Sandler, 1995).

What Teachers Can Do to Facilitate Meaningful Change in Grading and Reporting

1. Implement practices guided by knowledge rather than tradition or emotion.
2. Know the difference between accommodations and modifications.
3. Think big, but start small.
4. Initiate frequent, high-quality communication with families.

What Administrators Can Do

Although administrators have few opportunities to interact directly with struggling learners, they affect student learning indirectly in many ways, especially through their influence on teacher motivation and working conditions (Louis, Leithwood, Wahlstrom, & Anderson, 2010). Because of this influence, administrators play a vital role in implementing change in grading policies and practices. The importance of an administrator's interest, guidance, support, and encouragement cannot be underestimated. Furthermore, relatively small actions on the part of administrators can make a big difference in the success of implementation efforts.

1. Become Knowledgeable of Effective Grading and Reporting Practices

To lead successful change initiatives, administrators first must be knowledgeable about the elements of effective grading and reporting. Specifically, they must understand the shortcomings of many traditional grading practices; the importance of offering separate grades or marks for product, process, and process standards; and the crucial distinction between accommodations and modifications in standards for struggling learners. They also must be familiar with federal and state regulations regarding grading and reporting on the performance of struggling learners, as well as the implications of these regulations for district grading policies.

The key to developing this knowledge, of course, is to become skilled and comfortable in exploring the research on grading and reporting. Administrators need to become familiar with current studies on grading and reporting and with the implications of those investigations for better practice. Like teachers, they must be adept in searching the ERIC system and other established research databases so that they can guide effective change efforts.

Too often school leaders approach the challenge of grading reform by surveying what other school districts have done. They then collect examples of the report cards used in these other districts and form a committee to pick what they like from these examples in order to develop their own, new report card and reporting policies. What these leaders fail to recognize, however, is that the examples they gather from other districts were likely developed in exactly the same way: not from consideration of research on best practice, but from haphazard surveys of still other districts' practices. So instead of basing reforms on evidence of truly effective practice, they end up simply replicating the mistakes of others.

With the knowledge gained from exploring research databases, administrators can offer informed leadership in change initiatives. They can help plan professional development activities that focus on truly effective grading and reporting practices for struggling learners. Most important, they must become active participants in those activities, demonstrating to all that these issues are a priority for everyone concerned with helping students.

2. Purposefully Share the Advantages of Standards-Based Grading With All Stakeholders

One of the main reasons people resist change is that they do not understand the reasons behind the change or what benefits the change will bring. In addition, the old adage, "Why fix it if it isn't broken?" rings true to many educators and parents alike. In no aspect of education is this more prevalent than in grading and reporting. Tradition dictates practice in grading and reporting more than in any other area of education.

Because of the strong influence of tradition, administrators leading initiatives to reform grading policies and practices must make special efforts to inform all stakeholders about why change is essential and the specific advantages such change will bring. Teachers need to be made aware of the inadequacies of many current grading practices, especially with regard to struggling learners. Parents and guardians need to be informed of the benefits the changes will bring and of how more accurate and detailed information about their children's learning will allow them to become more supportive of their children and more engaged in the children's learning activities. Board members and community leaders also need to know the specific advantages of proposed changes in grading and reporting and how these changes will bring increased clarity and meaning to the reporting process.

3. Take an Active, Direct Role in Collaboratively Exploring Change Options With Teachers

Teachers take many cues from school administrators in deciding what is truly important in their district and particularly their school. These cues stem from administrators' active participation in professional development activities, from the topics they discuss in meetings, and from the questions they ask in brief hallway conversations. Administrators who merely introduce professional development sessions on grading struggling learners, for example, and then leave the sessions in order to deal with other school matters, communicate to teachers and staff members that those other matters are a higher priority. Administrators who help plan and organize professional learning opportunities related to grading and reporting, actively engage in those sessions, and then ensure that those implementing change initiatives have the resources and support necessary to succeed create a districtwide or schoolwide focus on purposeful improvement.

4. Support Teachers in Their Implementation Efforts

For change initiatives in grading and reporting for struggling learners to succeed, administrators must create the conditions and structures that support teachers' implementation efforts. This means that administrators must establish an environment of informed, collaborative leadership so that decisions can be based on shared knowledge of solid research evidence rather than on opinion or conjecture. They must broaden stakeholders' involvement in the decision-making process by keeping board members, other administrators, teachers, parents and guardians, and even students abreast of the changes being made and the reasons behind those changes. Most important, administrators must talk with teachers, listen to them, and interact with them regularly to enhance motivation. They also must create conditions in schools that prompt continued teacher collaboration and then provide the time and structures necessary for that collaboration to take place. This can be as simple as scheduling a time for follow-up meetings where teachers can discuss problems and share ideas on improvement strategies to going to higher-level administrators or board members to request additional support. Even if such requests are not granted, making them demonstrates to everyone a strong level of commitment to making things work.

What Administrators Can Do to Facilitate Meaningful Change in Grading and Reporting

1. Become knowledgeable of effective grading and reporting practices.
2. Purposefully share the advantages of standards-based grading with all stakeholders.
3. Take an active, direct role in collaboratively exploring change options with teachers.
4. Support teachers in their implementation efforts.

What Higher Education Institutions Can Do

To bring about truly meaningful change in grading and reporting for struggling learners, colleges and universities must make significant changes in their teacher preparation programs at both the undergraduate and graduate levels. Current evidence indicates that most teachers have scant knowledge of various grading methods, the advantages and shortcomings of each, or the effects of different grading policies on students' motivation to learn, especially the motivation of struggling learners. A major reason for this lack of knowledge is that most teacher preparation programs devote little if any attention to these topics (Brookhart & Nitko, 2008; Stiggins, 1993, 2008). With increasing proportions of struggling learners being served in general education classrooms, every teacher will be faced with the challenge of assigning fair and meaningful grades to these students.

Providing preservice and practicing teachers with the knowledge and practical experience they need to develop effective grading and reporting policies for struggling learners will require change in several aspects of teachers' preparation programs and professional development experiences (see Jung & Guskey, 2010b). Although these aspects are closely related, careful attention to each individually will be vital to success.

1. Make Information on Effective Grading Policies and Practices an Integral Part of Coursework

Those preparing to become teachers must be intimately familiar with the challenges associated with standards-based grading, distinguishing the three kinds of learning criteria (product, process, progress), and the Inclusive Grading Model (Jung & Guskey, 2010a). These topics should be addressed in courses on student assessment and instructional methods as well as in practica and student-teaching seminars. As part of their coursework, preservice teachers should read the literature on grading and reporting and should have structured opportunities to reflect on and discuss the implications for practice. In addition, they need to be able to identify the critical difference between accommodations and modifications and have experiences using these in planning instructional programs for all types of struggling learners.

In our professional development work with teachers, we find that many teaching veterans, including many special education teachers, do not truly understand the difference between accommodations and modifications. Few recognize, for example, that an accommodation in one subject area can be a modification in another subject area for the same student. All teachers, regardless of their teaching level or subject area specialty, need to understand these concepts fully, not only for high-quality grading and reporting but also for intervention planning and implementation.

2. Model Best Practices When Grading Student Performance in Teacher Preparation Programs

Preservice teachers need to be given opportunities to experience and observe high-quality grading policies and practices in their own learning. Teachers at all levels tend to teach as they were taught. They also grade as they were graded, replicating practices that they experienced as students with little thought given to potential consequences, either positive or negative (Campbell & Evans, 2000; Guskey, 2006a). For this reason, opportunities need to be embedded in courses, practica, and student teaching experiences for preservice teachers to identify and experience exemplary grading in practice. They should engage in detailed discussions about grading and reporting, interview cooperating teachers about the grading practices used in the classroom, and then prepare reflective, written comparisons, considering possible disparities with evidence on best practice gleaned from the research.

3. Embed the Task of Grading and Reporting on the Performance of Struggling Learners in Both Coursework and Student Teaching

Many teacher preparation programs require student teachers to gather data on an individual student's performance within the context of specific lessons and during the delivery of intervention plans. Programs should take this practice one step further by requiring student teachers to actually complete intervention plans, progress reports, and report cards as a part of their preparatory experience. If exemplary progress reporting forms and report cards are not available within the student's placement, the teacher preparation program should offer parallel forms more aligned with best practice for the students to use in order to gain this experience.

4. Provide Teachers With Specific and Directive Feedback on Their Grading Policies and Practices

In addition to offering high-quality, field-based experiences as part of their teacher preparation programs, college and university supervisors should provide preservice teachers with specific feedback on their grading and reporting practices. General feedback can be given to larger groups of preservice teachers through practica or student teaching seminars. These experiences provide an excellent forum for students to discuss the grading practices currently being used, how they could alter those practices in classrooms where they teach in the future, and how they might model exemplary practice. Additionally, college and university supervisors should provide specific, individual feedback to preservice teachers as they practice grading and reporting during field-based experiences to ensure that what they are doing truly reflects exemplary practice.

5. Partner With Districts and Schools to Discuss and Improve Grading Policies and Practices

Colleges and universities must work with schools and school districts to review current grading and reporting policies and practices and to initiate reform efforts. The policies in place in most schools and districts today are based primarily on tradition and are woefully inadequate. They remain in place simply because, "We've always done it that way" (Guskey & Bailey, 2010). To ensure that policies and practices truly reflect best practice, higher education institutions must work collaboratively with schools and school districts, openly discussing the implications of current practice and exploring other, more positive options.

What Higher Education Institutions Can Do to Facilitate Meaningful Change in Grading and Reporting

1. Make information on effective grading policies and practices an integral part of coursework.
2. Model best practices when grading student performance in teacher preparation programs.
3. Embed the task of grading and reporting on the performance of struggling learners in both coursework and student teaching.
4. Provide teachers with specific and directive feedback on their grading policies and practices.
5. Partner with districts and schools to discuss and improve grading policies and practices.

One way to accomplish this is to identify teacher leaders who are using high-quality grading practices in their classrooms, and then provide them with a forum to discuss their ideas with colleagues (Reeves, 2008). These teacher leaders also could be invited to present their ideas in teacher preparation courses, describing their experiences and offering suggestions for implementation. Colleges and universities are uniquely situated to facilitate this kind of collaborative leadership and effectively prompt significant change in grading policies and practices at all levels.

Summary

Change is never easy. It is especially difficult when the change involves challenging long-held traditions. But when those traditions lie in opposition to current knowledge about best practice and may actually bring harm to students, especially those who are struggling learners, pressing for and facilitating change is imperative.

Each of the three levels of change we describe in this chapter has a unique and powerful influence. Changes in what teachers do, what administrators do, and what institutions of higher education do are all essential for meaningful improvement in grading and reporting on the performance of struggling learners. But as we noted, these levels of influence are intertwined, and each level can influence the others. The expressed needs of teachers and administrators, for example, often serve as feedback to higher education institutions that then initiate changes in preservice teacher education and leadership preparation programs. In turn, changes in college and university programs influence the knowledge and skills that teachers and administrators bring to their professional positions, helping them to improve their effectiveness. Because of this interrelatedness, no level can succeed in isolation on its own. In addition, no level can be neglected.

Improvement efforts, therefore, must be multifaceted and must approach change from a systemic perspective, addressing change at all three levels simultaneously. They also must be guided by the unified purpose of providing more accurate and more meaningful grading procedures for all students and particularly those who are struggling learners. Only those efforts that integrate changes in the actions of teachers, administrators, and institutions of higher education are likely to attain a high level of success and be sustained over time.

7

Frequently Asked Questions About Grading Struggling Learners

In previous chapters we described the challenges involved in assigning fair, accurate, and meaningful grades to struggling learners. We also outlined specific strategies educators can use to meet those challenges, as well as ways to adapt the strategies to particular contexts and to students' individual learning needs. Although we did our best to present these challenges and strategies concisely, it is likely that questions still remain. Some of these questions may involve issues that we mentioned earlier but did not discuss in great depth. Others might relate to aspects of the research on grading or distinctive implementation issues that are relevant only in specific contexts. Because of the importance of these issues to many educators, we want to address those questions here in hopes of clarifying our meaning, broadening understanding, and facilitating success in implementation efforts.

We have not arranged these questions in any particular order. Our goal was simply to cover the broadest range of potential concerns. In doing so, we recognize that not all of the questions will be relevant to every reader. Therefore in approaching the chapter, please feel free to read first those sections most relevant to your concerns and needs and then turn to other sections later. We hope that addressing these questions in some depth will clarify any issues that remain unresolved and enhance the practical knowledge of educators engaged in implementing standards-based grading and reporting, especially as it involves struggling learners.

1. Must all struggling learners have an individualized education program (IEP)?

Struggling learners come in many different forms and may be classified in many different ways. Some will be exceptional and have special learning needs that require the development of individualized education programs or IEPs. But such students represent only a small portion of those who may be considered "struggling."

Throughout this book we have stressed that struggling learners include not only those with identified special needs but also those students who may be English learners (ELs), students who have 504 plans, students receiving the highest and most intense level of intervention in a Response to Intervention (RTI) model, and other students who are experiencing difficulty learning a specific concept or skill or mastering a particular standard at their grade level. All such students may be considered to be struggling learners who require support and adaptations to grade-level standards.

We hasten to add, however, that we also consider classification as an exceptional or struggling learner to be both flexible and temporary. Within a subject area or course, an individual student may struggle with some skills but not with others. In addition, that student might struggle with a particular standard during one marking period and require some form of modification. But with appropriate intervention, that student's learning problem might be rectified, allowing the student to return to grade-level work and no longer be considered struggling. From our perspective then, "struggling learner" implies any student who is experiencing a learning difficulty or set of difficulties with respect to particular standards and for whom some adaptations in the standards might be needed.

2. Who decides if a student is a struggling learner?

As is true with most instructional decisions regarding individual students, the classroom teacher has a crucial role in determining whether or not an individual student is considered a struggling learner and in need of support and modification to the learning standards. But teachers never act alone in making these important decisions. For students with disabilities, schools follow specific procedures that align with the federal requirements of the Individuals with Disabilities Education Act. For other struggling learners, a team typically decides the nature of a student's learning difficulties and what kind of modification in particular standards might be needed. This team includes fellow teachers, specialists, those who conducted the assessments, school administrators, parents, the student, and anyone the student or parent wishes to involve (IDEIA, 2004).

The team collaborates to make decisions about what modification in the standards would be most appropriate for the student, how those modifications will be implemented in the student's instructional program, what supports are needed, who will provide supports, how progress will be assessed, and how results will be reported. The team also will be involved in reviewing the student's learning progress, determining the effectiveness of the intervention in which the student is involved, and deciding when modifications need to be revised or are no longer necessary. Because of teachers' close contact with students and primary role in directing students' instructional programs, however, their input in all of these decisions remains critical. For this reason teachers must make sure to closely monitor students' learning progress so that decisions can be made based on the most accurate, timely, and valid evidence available.

3. What is the most important first step to take in implementing standards-based grading?

As we described in Chapter 2, the essential first step in reforming grading and reporting at any level of education is to define the purpose of grading and to make explicit the meaning of grades. No change in grading policy or method can succeed in the absence of a clearly defined purpose. At the school level, this means that building leaders must engage all teachers and staff members in focused discussions about why we grade, for whom the information is intended, and what the desired results are. To our knowledge, no definitive research has established any single purpose as "best." Nevertheless, compelling evidence shows that consensus among the educators in a school or district regarding the purpose of grades and grading is essential to success.

To emphasize the importance of a clearly defined purpose, we recommend that a purpose statement be included on the first page of every report card. In a special box or highlighted area, a statement should be printed that begins: "The purpose of this report card is . . . ." A clear and concise purpose statement helps all stakeholders recognize the report card's specific intent. It also provides the basis for developing the content and form of the report card. Most important, it establishes a premise for defending or justifying the grades and marks that are assigned.

Most of the problems that educators experience in implementing reforms in grading and reporting, and especially those encountered in revising report cards, can be traced to an ill-defined purpose or the lack of any purpose statement whatsoever. Although reaching consensus on the purpose of a grade or the report card can be a difficult and trying experience, it remains the essential first step.

4. What is the most important first step to take in implementing standards-based grading for struggling learners?

Once a standards-based report card has been developed and rubrics established for assigning standards-based grades or marks, procedures must be set for determining which standards need accommodations, which need modifications, and what form those accommodations or modifications will take for each struggling learner. Recall, the Inclusive Grading Model we presented in Chapter 3 was designed explicitly for this purpose. The model sets forth a specific series of steps for educators to take in making these important decisions. By following the model's five steps, educators will be able to guarantee that (1) struggling learners have an instructional program that is appropriate to their specific needs and (2) their performance on all standards, including any standards that have been modified, is reported clearly and accurately. In addition, the model allows teachers to communicate this pertinent information to families in a manner that can be used to guide improvement efforts. It effectively and efficiently removes barriers between home and school and ensures that teachers' and parents' efforts to help struggling learners remain coordinated and harmonious.

5. How are standards-based report cards different from traditional report cards?

Standards-based report cards differ from traditional report cards in two important ways. First, they require teachers to base grades or marks on explicit criteria derived from the articulated learning standards. When assigning grades, teachers must analyze the meaning of each standard and decide what evidence best reflects achievement of that specific standard. As a result, standards-based report cards offer multiple grades or marks for each subject area or course of study. In other words, instead of a single, overall grade that combines information from a variety of learning outcomes, teachers assign separate grades for each reporting standard. This offers families, as well as students, more detailed information on specific learning strengths and on areas where learning difficulties may be evident.

The second way standards-based report cards differ is that they compel teachers to distinguish *product*, *process*, and *progress* criteria in assigning grades or marks. As we described in Chapter 2, product criteria reflect students' academic achievement and performance. They focus on what students know and are able to do at a particular point in time. Process criteria reflect how students reached their level of achievement or proficiency. They typically relate to students' work habits, study skills, class behaviors, or effort. Progress criteria are based on how much students gain from their learning experiences or how much improvement has been made. Other names for progress criteria include *learning gain, value-added learning,* and *educational growth.* By providing separate grades or marks for product, process, and progress criteria, standards-based report cards not only clarify the meaning of the grades assigned; they also provide a more complete and comprehensive description of students' performance in school.

6. Will implementing standards-based report cards improve student learning, especially that of struggling learners?

Of all the questions we are asked with regard to standards-based reporting, this is undoubtedly the most frequent. It is also the question for which we have the least definitive answer.

Admittedly, at this time we know of no well-designed, systematic studies that have linked the implementation of standards-based report cards to improvements in student learning. That is to say that to our knowledge, there is neither confirmation that such a link exists nor strong evidence to show that it does not. Although such studies may be forthcoming, we know of none that have yet been conducted and their results reported.

In a larger sense, however, why would we expect changing the report card to affect student learning in any way, positive or negative? Changing the way we report information on student learning has no direct or immediate effect on what students learn or how they are taught. Any potential impact on curriculum or instruction would be tangential at best. So why would we expect standards-based report cards to influence student learning?

From our perspective, standards-based reporting is more about communicating better and more accurate information to families and students *in order to provide the basis for improving student learning.* Whether or not this leads to specific improvements depends not on the information itself but on how that information is used.

Another way to think about this issue is to see it as analogous to improving performance in a sporting event. If we were to tell you the score of a game you were playing, would that help you play better? Probably not. Similarly, if we were to tell you that in the game, these are the things you are doing well and these are the things you need to improve, would that alone improve your play? Also probably not. But if we were truly interested in working together to improve your performance, which of these two different types of information is likely to be more helpful? Obviously, it is the latter.

That is what standards-based reporting does. Instead of offering only a nebulous, overall indicator of performance (i.e., the score of the game), it provides families and students with detailed information on school performance so that improvement efforts can be more targeted and effective. This is especially relevant for the families of struggling learners who want and need specific guidance in their efforts to help their children improve.

7. If schools implement standards-based grading, will the grades and marks assigned to struggling learners likely go up or down?

In our experience, schools implementing standards-based grading and standards-based report cards generally have seen no difference in the *average* grades of students in particular classes or in the entire school. Nevertheless, it is likely changes will occur in the grades or marks of individual students. Since approximately the same number of students will see improvements as see declines, when combined these changes average out.

As we noted earlier, some students receive passing grades simply because they are compliant and well behaved, turn in assignments on time, and do whatever the teacher asks, even though they may not demonstrate proficiency on grade-level standards. When such process elements are removed from the product or achievement grade and reported separately in a standards-based format, the academic achievement grades assigned to these students are likely to be lower.

On the other hand, if teachers recognize that grade-level standards are unattainable for particular struggling learners and take appropriate steps to modify the standards so that they are more in line with those students' levels of performance and academic history, grades and marks may actually improve. It would be noted, of course, that these grades are based on modified standards. Still, it would serve to make the grades a fairer and more honest depiction of students' actual performance in school.

8. Should the number of times a student requires retesting or additional chances to demonstrate proficiency be considered in determining a grade or mark?

Again, to answer this question we must return to the stated purpose. Is your purpose in grading and reporting to describe accurately what students know and are able to do at a particular point in time? Or is it to describe how they got to that level of performance (i.e., how many attempts they made prior to success)? If it is truly the former, then how students reached that level is insignificant and should not be considered in determining their grade or mark. The grades represent an accurate depiction of students' level of proficiency with regard to particular standards at the time of reporting.

Most people know, for example, that Thomas Edison invented the lightbulb. It is what he achieved at a particular point in time. Few people know that in the process of creating the lightbulb, he had over 1,000 failed experiments before succeeding. Nor do they care. We believe that if you want to report on the "process" of reaching the standard or goal, you must keep that separate from a grade or mark that is supposed to be a fair and accurate indicator of whether or not the goal was met.

9. What grades or marks are included on the permanent record or transcript of struggling learners?

Guidelines for what is included in students' permanent records or recorded on transcripts vary widely from school to school and district to district. Schools using traditional report cards typically include only a single, overall grade for each subject area or course, derived in most cases from an average of the grades or marks assigned in each reporting period of the school year. Some schools include the grades assigned during each reporting period in addition to an overall grade, although this tends to complicate documents that many educators believe should present only a general summary of performance.

Schools using standards-based report cards typically report summary grades or marks *for each reporting standard*. That means that students' permanent records and transcripts include four to six grades or marks for each subject area or course of study, one for each of the specified reporting standards. Typically these standards are briefly labeled on the record or transcript so that those receiving the information can interpret the meaning of each mark. Some secondary schools also include an overall, summary course grade with the individual reporting standard marks.

An important difference in the permanent records and transcripts of schools using standards-based report cards relates to how summary grades or marks are determined. Schools using standards-based report cards *always base overall, summary grades or marks on the most recent evidence,* never on an average of marks across marking periods. The defining purpose of standards-based reporting is to reflect accurately what students have learned and are able to do at a specific point in time. The most valid evidence for this purpose is clearly the most current or recent evidence. Using an average that includes past evidence that is no longer indicative of students' true level of performance distorts and invalidates the grades' meaning.

The permanent records or transcripts of struggling learners are much the same. The only difference would be the designation of grades or marks that have been based on modified expectations. The details of how the standards have been modified would *not* be included in the permanent record or on the transcript. Instead, these would be noted elsewhere in documents provided for the students' families. It is legal to indicate in permanent records or transcripts that a modification was made to the standards (see Jung & Guskey, 2010a). It also enhances the accuracy and honesty of the included information.

10. What is the best way to designate modified standards on the permanent record or transcript?

We recommend noting modified standards on permanent records and transcripts the same way it is done on the report card: by placing an asterisk (*) or some other symbol by the grade or mark and then indicating on the form that this means the grade or mark is based on modified standards. No other information regarding the nature of the modification is needed.

Including such a notation is imperative when the standards have been modified. Standards-based reporting requires honesty and accuracy in the information communicated. To base a grade or mark on standards that have been modified and not report this fact conveys false information. As we have stressed throughout this book, when standards are modified to make them more appropriate for the performance level of students, this must be noted in some way on the report card as well as in the permanent record and the transcript.

11. What grades are used to determine course credit or promotion to the next grade level?

As we noted earlier, one of the ways standards-based report cards differ from traditional reporting forms is that they compel teachers to distinguish product, process, and progress criteria in assigning grades or marks. While each of these types of criteria and learning goals is important, when it comes to course credit or promotion from one grade level to the next, most schools rely exclusively on academic achievement and performance data. In other words, they use only information on the attainment of product goals that relate to students' performance on the articulated grade level or course standards. The same is true for determining students' athletic eligibility for middle school or high school sports.

A related question is whether or not the decision process is altered for exceptional and struggling learners who are working toward modified expectations. Again, in most cases, schools base the decision solely on students' performance related to product goals and standards, but they do so based on those standards deemed most appropriate for the student. If a student performs well on standards that have been modified, course credit and promotion are granted, but the modification is then noted on the permanent record and transcript. In this way, students are still expected to meet specific learning standards in order to gain course credit and be promoted, but these decisions are based on performance on the standards determined by educators to be most appropriate for those students.

12. What is the best way to inform parents of the reasons for moving to standards-based grading?

Parents and guardians can be some of the strongest advocates for standards-based grading and the use of standards-based report cards. They can also be some of the most adamant opponents. Many parents are comfortable with traditional report cards that offer a single grade for each subject or course. They understand these forms, or believe that they do, because such forms closely resemble the report cards they received when they were in school two or three decades ago. Standards-based report cards challenge parents' comfort simply because they are different. Some parents even fear that changing the report card so drastically might be potentially harmful to their child's success both in school and beyond.

The parents and guardians of struggling learners, however, typically have a very different perspective. Many of them find traditional report cards to be meaningless. The low grades their child receives only confirm what they already know: that their child is, indeed, struggling. A single overall grade tells them nothing about the learning goals on which their child's performance was judged, areas that might be unique strengths, or areas of difficulty. In addition, traditional report cards give families no guidance or direction as to how they might help, even if they are highly committed to offering whatever assistance might be needed.

In our experience, parents and guardians can become powerful allies in implementing standards-based report cards if they are made aware of why the change is being made and what advantages such change will bring. Some schools accomplish this early in the implementation process by involving parents and guardians on development teams. The parents of struggling learners can be particularly helpful in this way. In other schools, teachers and building leaders use school council meetings or parent/teacher association (PTA) meetings to explain the rationale behind the development of the new report card, share draft versions, and solicit parent input.

One of the most effective approaches we have used is to begin implementation by sending home to families two report cards: the traditional one currently in use and the newly developed standards-based reporting form. Typically we do this for two reporting periods so that families can see students' progress on the standards. We then survey parents and guardians, asking them what they like and do not like about each form, and which form they would prefer receiving. In every instance the overwhelming majority of parents chose the standards-based reporting form. And because of the detailed information offered in the standards-based form, the parents and guardians of struggling learners often become some of the strongest advocates.

13. What is the best way to encourage parents to make comments on the report card?

As we emphasized in Chapter 6, every standards-based report card should be designed to include a section that requests comments from parents or guardians as well as students. This gives families the chance to raise questions or to seek additional clarification of any information included on the report card. It also encourages family involvement in learning and shows parents that teachers and school leaders value their comments and input.

Occasionally, however, teachers find that parents are reluctant to offer comments. Report cards are returned with a parent's or guardian's signature but nothing more. In some cases schools try to resolve this by listing a series of statements or questions about the report card and asking parents or guardians simply to check any that apply. One question nearly all include asks families if they would like to schedule a parent/teacher conference to discuss the report card. Although helpful, this approach significantly restricts the scope of responses families might provide.

In our experience, two reasons account for families' reluctance to offer more detailed, written comments. The first is parents' and guardians' uncertainty about how their questions or comments will be received by teachers. Questioning a teacher about how a particular grade or mark was determined might be seen as challenging the teacher's judgment or authority. Teachers who feel this way might then be harsher in judging their child's performance in the future, jeopardizing the chances of success.

To waylay this fear, teachers need to stress their openness to parents' and guardians' comments and actively encourage the expression of questions or concerns. Some teachers do this during open house meetings or parent/teacher conferences. Other teachers send personal notes to parents or use follow-up phone calls after report cards are sent home.

A second reason for the reluctance to make comments relates to parents' and guardians' uncertainty or lack of confidence in their own language or writing abilities. Some parents' educational backgrounds left them with limited skills in written expression. Adding comments on a report card would not only reveal these limitations, it might prove embarrassing to their child, and no parent or guardian wants to do that. Likewise, the families of students who are English learners often feel uncomfortable about their own limited English skills. Even those who are fairly competent in oral language often struggle with writing.

Teachers need to make special efforts to alleviate such concerns. Open house meetings and parent/teacher conferences provide an opportunity to interact with these parents when they are able to attend. Personal notes and phone calls can be useful as well. But in some cases, teachers need to make special efforts to meet with parents or guardians at times that suit the family's schedule, or even visit the family's home. These types of interactions do wonders to break down the communication barriers between homes and schools. They also show parents and guardians the commitment of educators to the learning success of their children.

14. What if a student needs modifications on most or all standards? Do I need an IEP goal or intervention plan for every modification?

No. For students who need most standards modified, teams should prioritize the standards and select the 6 to 10 outcomes they want to be the focus. Certainly, that does not mean that the student's educational experience is limited to those 6 to 10 outcomes. The instructional team will work to provide that student with access to the entire general curriculum. However, for reporting purposes, it is important to decide the criteria by which proficiency will be measured. Teams still must decide *what to measure*. Taking Jimi as an example, the team may agree that all or nearly all of the reporting standards need modification. For Jimi's IEP, the team may collapse those by subject area and have one IEP goal for each subject. Or they may group standards in some other way for his IEP. Jimi will also likely have IEP goals that are not directly tied to a general curriculum standard, such as goals for his social skills. On the report card, teams can note if any standards were not assessed.

It should be noted, however, that very few students need *all* standards to be modified. Even most students with disabilities will be working toward grade-level standards in most of their coursework. For other students who may need modifications across all areas, many will need these modifications only temporarily. Carlos, for example, likely needed most areas modified when he first arrived in the United States, but he will need fewer and fewer modifications in the future and eventually will need none.

15. What if after adaptations are in place a student fails? Is it legal for ELs and students with IEPs or 504 plans to receive a failing grade?

Any student, exceptional or otherwise, can legally fail a subject or course. The important distinction with exceptional learners is why the failure occurred. Legal provisions stipulate that IEPs must provide students with disabilities the opportunity to receive passing grades and advance in grade level with their peers (*Board of Education v. Rowley,* 1982). This litigation yielded two important implications for schools. First, no student may fail because needed services were not provided. If a student with a disability or an English learner fails a class, the school must be prepared to demonstrate that appropriate supports were provided. Otherwise, a failing grade may be seen as an indication of failure on the part of the school, not as the student's failure (*Board of Education v. Rowley,* 1982). Second, a student should not fail on a standard that the education team determined was unattainable for that student. Instead, individualized goals should be written in the IEP, 504 plan, or EL plan based on the level of work the student is able to complete successfully. If appropriate services and supports are in place and the appropriate level of work is assessed, then the same range of grades available to all students is applicable to exceptional learners, including failing grades.

16. Can report cards legally identify the student's status as a struggling learner?

The U.S. Department of Education's Office of Civil Rights (OCR) has provided guidance in the area of report cards and transcripts for struggling learners (2008). The OCR sees the purpose of both report cards and transcripts as reporting students' achievement, but it differentiates the consumers of these reports. Report cards communicate information about students' achievement with the student, parents, and teachers and should not be shared outside of these groups by the school. Transcripts, on the other hand, are shared with other schools, with employers, and with institutes of higher education. Because of third-party sharing, rules of confidentiality apply to transcripts that do not apply to report cards. If considered necessary for the purpose of accuracy, a student's EL status or the fact that the student had an IEP or 504 plan may be indicated on the report card (Freedman, 2000). Schools, however, must carefully review whether such information is truly necessary for a student. There would be no need, for example, to remind the family of a student with multiple disabilities every nine weeks that their child qualifies for special education.

17. Is it legal for transcripts to identify the curriculum as being modified?

Perhaps the most common of all reporting myths is that modifications to the standards by which a student was graded may not be noted on any student's transcript. Under the Individuals With

Disabilities Education Act (IDEA) of 1997 and its reauthorization (IDEIA, 2004), Section 504 of the Rehabilitation Act of 1973, and the Americans With Disabilities Act Amendments Act of 2008, transcripts may not identify students as having a disability. However, noting a "modified" curriculum is legal, as long as modifications are available to any student who needs them. In other words, if modifications are available to students with disabilities, English learners, and other struggling students, then noting a standard as having been modified on the transcript is legal and a practice we recommend.

18. Do high school students requiring modifications receive course credit toward a diploma? Do modifications make a student ineligible for athletics?

Once the Inclusive Grading Model is implemented, many questions about policy arise. Some schools may choose to include policies about the precise number of modifications allowed in order for a student to be eligible for a particular type of diploma or for athletic participation and so on. To answer these questions, we suggest that leaders consider the purpose of each of these. What is the purpose, for example, for requiring certain grades for participation in athletics? Is the purpose to ensure all athletes are working toward grade-level standards? Or would it be appropriate to include all students who are performing well on the level of work they are capable of completing? Similarly, as districts consider requirements for distinctions and diplomas, the same questions must be considered. What is the purpose of requiring a certain grade point average? Is it to communicate that students mastered a particular level of work? Or is it something else? We have opinions on these questions, but the answers are left ultimately to school policy makers.

Conclusion

The challenges involved in assigning fair, accurate, and meaningful grades to struggling learners in a standards-based environment are many and complex. They test the will and dedication of the most determined educators. But while serious and daunting, these challenges are not insurmountable. Meeting them will require a firm understanding of the knowledge base, the courage to challenge long-held traditions, and a strong and abiding commitment to doing what is truly best for students at every level of education.

We have done our best in this book to offer that necessary understanding of the knowledge base in grading and reporting. We have also tried to describe guidelines stemming from that knowledge base for improved practice. As we noted many times, much of what is written about assigning grades or marks to struggling learners is based more on opinion and conjecture than on valid evidence of what is most honest and effective. We hope we have provided a useful summary of that evidence and offered helpful suggestions on how it can lead to better policies and practices. The necessary courage and commitment, however, must come from you.

We remain convinced the gap between our knowledge base and practice is greater in grading and reporting than in any other area of education. The only way we know to reduce that gap is to question those long-held traditions and push hard for practices known to be more effective. If the ideas we presented here prompt those questions and inspire a commitment among educators at all levels to do better, then we will consider our efforts a success.

References

Adelman, C. (1999). *Answers in the tool box: Academic intensity, attendance patterns, and bachelor's degree attainment.* Washington, DC: Office of Educational Research and Improvement, U.S. Department of Education.

Baird, S. M. (1994). *Intervention plan.* Unpublished document, Auburn University, Auburn, Alabama.

Baker, E. T., Wang, M. C., & Walberg, H. J. (1995). The effects of inclusion on learning. *Educational Leadership, 52*(4), 33–35.

Board of Education v. Rowley, 458 U.S. 176 (1982).

Bolt, D. M., Ysseldyke, J., & Patterson, M. J. (2010). Students, teachers, and schools as sources of variability, integrity, and sustainability in implementing progress monitoring. *School Psychology Review, 39*(4), 612–630.

Brookhart, S. M. (1991). Grading practices and validity. *Educational Measurement: Issues and Practice, 10*(1), 35–36.

Brookhart, S. M. (1993). Teachers' grading practices: Meaning and values. *Journal of Educational Measurement, 30*(2), 123–142.

Brookhart, S. M., & Nitko. A. J. (2008). *Assessment and grading in classrooms.* Upper Saddle River, NJ: Pearson Education.

Bursuck, W. D., Munk, D. D., & Olson, M. M. (1999). The fairness of report card grading adaptations: What do students with and without disabilities think? *Remedial and Special Education, 20,* 84–92.

Bursuck, W., Polloway, E. A., Plante, L., Epstein, M. H., Jayanthi, M., & McConeghy, J. (1996). Report card grading and adaptations: A national survey of classroom practices. *Exceptional Children, 62*(2), 301–318.

Campbell, C., & Evans, J. (2000). Investigation of preservice teachers' classroom assessment practices during student teaching. *Journal of Educational Research, 93*(2), 350–355.

Carlberg, C., & Kavale, K. A. (1980). The efficacy of special versus regular class placement for exceptional children: A meta-analysis. *Journal of Special Education, 14,* 296–309.

Cizek, G. J., Fitzgerald, S. M., & Rachor, R. E. (1996). Teachers' assessment practices: Preparation, isolation, and the kitchen sink. *Educational Assessment, 3*(2), 159–179.

Council of Chief State School Officers & National Governors Association Center for Best Practices (CCSSO). (2010). *Common core state standards initiative.* Washington, DC: Author. Retrieved from http://www.corestandards.org/Standards/K12/

Cross, L. H., & Frary, R. B. (1996, April). *Hodgepodge grading: Endorsed by students and teachers alike.* Paper presented at the annual meeting of the National Council on Measurement in Education, New York, NY.

Data Accountability Center. (n.d.). *Part B child count,* 2008. Retrieved from http://www.ideadata.org/PartBChildCount.asp

Donahue, K., & Zigmond, N. (1990). Academic grades of ninth-grade urban learning disabled students and low-achieving peers. *Exceptionality, 1*(1), 17–27.

Dyal, A., Carpenter, L., & Wright, J. V. (2009). Assistive technology: What every school leader should know. *Education, 129*(3), 556–560.

Engelmann, S. (1999). The benefits of direct instruction: Affirmative action for at-risk students. *Educational Leadership, 57*(1), 77.

Esty, W. W., & Teppo, A. R. (1992). Grade assignment based on progressive improvement. *Mathematics Teacher, 85*(8), 616–618.

Etscheidt, S. K. (2006). Progress monitoring: Legal issues and recommendations for IEP teams. *Teaching Exceptional Children, 38(3),* 56–60.

Frary, R. B., Cross, L. H., & Weber, L. J. (1993). Testing and grading practices and opinions of secondary teachers of academic subjects: Implications for instruction in measurement. *Educational measurement: Issues and Practices, 12*(3), 23–30.

Freedman, M. K. (2000). *Testing, grading, and granting diplomas to special education students.* Special Report No. 18. Horsham, PA: LRP.

Freedman, M. K. (2005). *Student testing and the law: The requirements educators, parents, and officials should know.* Horsham, PA: LRP.

Friedman, S. J., & Frisbie, D. A. (1995). The influence of report cards on the validity of grades reported to parents. *Educational and Psychological Measurement, 55*(1), 5–26.

Friedman, S. J., & Manley, M. (1992). Improving high school grading practices: Experts vs. practitioners. *NASSP Bulletin, 76*(544), 100–104.

Fuchs, L. S., Fuchs, D., & Hollenbeck, K. N. (2007). Extending responsiveness to intervention to mathematics at first and third grades. *Learning Disabilities Research & Practice, 22*(1), 13–24.

Gersten, R., Vaughn, S., & Brengelman, S. U. (1996). Grading and academic feedback for special education students and students with learning difficulties. In T. R. Guskey (Ed.), *Communicating student learning: 1996 yearbook of the Association for Supervision and Curriculum and Development* (pp. 47–57). Alexandria, VA: Association for Supervision and Curriculum Development.

Gotlieb, M. (2006). *Assessing English language learners: Bridges from language proficiency to academic achievement.* Thousand Oaks, CA: Corwin.

Guskey, T. R. (2002a). Computerized gradebooks and the myth of objectivity. *Phi Delta Kappan, 83*(10), 775–780.

Guskey, T. R. (2002b). *How's my kid doing? A parents' guide to grades, marks, and report cards.* San Francisco: Jossey-Bass.

Guskey, T. R. (2004). The communication challenge of standards-based reporting. *Phi Delta Kappan, 86*(4), 326–329.

Guskey, T. R. (2006a). "It wasn't fair!" Educators' recollections of their experiences as students with grading. *Journal of Educational Research and Policy Studies, 6*(2), 111–124.

Guskey, T. R. (2006b). Making high school grades meaningful. *Phi Delta Kappan, 87*(9), 670–675.

Guskey, T. R. (Ed.). (2009). *Practical solutions for serious problems in standards-based grading.* Thousand Oaks, CA: Corwin.

Guskey, T. R., & Anderman, E. M. (2008). Students at bat. *Educational Leadership, 66*(3), 8–14.

Guskey, T. R., & Bailey, J. M. (2001). *Developing grading and reporting systems for student learning.* Thousand Oaks, CA: Corwin.

Guskey, T. R., & Bailey, J. M. (2010). *Developing standards-based report cards.* Thousand Oaks, CA: Corwin.

Hattie, J., & Timperley, H. (2007). The power of feedback. *Review of Educational Research, 77*(1), 81–112.

Henderson, A., & Berla, N. (Eds.) (1994). *A new generation of evidence: The family is critical to student achievement.* Washington, DC: National Committee for Citizens in Education.

Herring, W. L., McGrath, D., & Buckley, J. (2006). *Demographic and school characteristics of students receiving special education in the elementary grades.* Washington, DC: National Center for Education Statistics.

Hoover-Dempsey, K., & Sandler, H. (1995). Parental involvement in children's education: Why does it make a difference? *Teachers College Record, 97*(2), 310–331.

Horowitz, S. H. (2006). *Checking up on learning disabilities* Retrieved from http://www.ncld.org/ld-basics/ld-explained/basic-facts/checking-up-on-learning-disabilities

Hunt, P., Farron-Davis, F., Beckstead, S., Curtis, D., & Goetz, L. (1994). Evaluating the effects of placement of students with severe disabilities in general education versus special classes. *Journal of the Association for Persons With Severe Handicaps, 19*, 200–214.

Individuals With Disabilities Education Act (IDEA), 20 U.S.C. §§ 1400 to 1491 (1997).

Individuals With Disabilities Education Improvement Act (IDEIA), 20 U.S.C. §§ 1400 to 1482 (2004).

Jung, L. A. (2009). The challenges of grading and reporting in special education: An inclusive grading model. In T. R. Guskey (Ed.), *Practical solutions for serious problems in standards-based grading* (pp. 27–40). Thousand Oaks, CA: Corwin.

Jung, L. A. (2010). Can embedding prompts in the IFSP form improve the quality of IFSPs developed? *Journal of Early Intervention, 32*(3), 200–213.

Jung, L. A., & Guskey, T. R. (2007). Standards-based grading and reporting: A model for special education. *Teaching Exceptional Children, 40*(2), 48–53.

Jung, L. A., & Guskey, T. R. (2010a). Grading exceptional learners. *Educational Leadership, 67*(5), 31–35.

Jung, L. A., & Guskey, T. R. (2010b). Preparing teachers for grading students with learning disabilities. *Insights on Learning Disabilities, 7*(2), 43–53.

Jung, L. A. & Swan, G. M. (June, 2011). Making the most of progress monitoring. *Educational Leadership, 68*, online.

Jung, L. A., Baird, S. M., Gomez, C, & Galyon-Keramidas, C. (2008). Family-centered intervention: Bridging the gap between IEPs and implementation. *Teaching Exceptional Children, 41*(1), 26–33.

Kutash, K., Duchnowski, A. J., & Lynn, N. (2009). The use of evidence-based instructional strategies in special education settings in secondary schools: Development, implementation and outcomes. *Teaching & Teacher Education, 25*(6), 917–923.

Louis, K. S., Leithwood, K., Wahlstrom, K. L., & Anderson, S. E. (2010, July). *Learning from leadership: Investigating the links to improve student learning.* Minneapolis, MN: Center for Applied Research and Educational Improvement, University of Minnesota; and Toronto: ON: Ontario Institute for Studies in Education, University of Toronto. Retrieved from http://www.wallacefoundation.org/KnowledgeCenter/KnowledgeTopics/CurrentAreasofFocus/EducationalLeadership/Pages/learning-from-leadership-investigating-the-links-to-improved-student-learning.aspx

McMillan, J. H. (2001). Secondary teachers' classroom assessment and grading practices. *Educational Measurement: Issues and Practice, 20*(1), 20–32.

McMillan, J. H., Myran, S., & Workman, D. (2002). Elementary teachers' classroom assessment and grading practices. *Journal of Educational Research, 95*(4), 203–213.

Mellard, D. F., & Johnson, E. (2008). *RTI: A practitioner's guide to implementing response to intervention.* Thousand Oaks, CA: Corwin.

Mellard, D. F., McKnight, M., & Woods, K. (2009). Response to intervention screening and progress-monitoring practices in 41 local schools. *Learning Disabilities Research & Practice, 24*(4), 186–195.

National Council of Teachers of Mathematics. (1989). *Curriculum and evaluation standards for school mathematics.* Reston, VA: Author.

Natriello, G., Riehl, C. J., & Pallas, A. M. (1994). *Between the rock of standards and the hard place of accommodation: Evaluation practices of teachers in high schools serving disadvantaged students.* Baltimore, MD: Center for Research on Effective Schooling for Disadvantaged Students, Johns Hopkins University.

Nava, F. J. G., & Loyd, B. H. (1992, April). *An investigation of achievement and nonachievement criteria in elementary and secondary school grading.* Paper presented at the annual meeting of the American Educational Research Association, San Francisco, CA.

No Child Left Behind Act, 20 U.S.C. §§ 6301 *et seq.* (2008).

Office of Civil Rights. (2008, October 17). *Dear colleague letter: Report cards and transcripts for students with disabilities.* Retrieved from www.ed.gov/about/offices/list/ocr/letters/colleague-20081017.html

Ornstein, A. C. (1994). Grading practices and policies: And overview and some suggestions. *NASSP Bulletin, 78*(559), 55–64.

Polloway, E. A., Epstein, M. H., Bursuck, W. D., Roderique, T. W., McConeghy, J. L., & Jayanthi, M. (1994). Classroom grading: A national survey of policies. *Remedial and Special Education, 15,* 162–170.

Reeves, D. (2008). Effective grading. *Educational Leadership, 65*(5), 85–87.

Rehabilitation Act of 1973, 29 U.S.C. 794 § 504.

Ring, M. M., & Reetz, L. (2000). Modification effects on attribution of middle school students with learning disabilities. *Learning Disabilities Research & Practice, 15,* 34–42.

Schmid, C. F. (1954). *Handbook of graphic presentation*. New York, NY: Ronald Press.

Silva, M., Munk, D. D., & Bursuck, W. D. (2005). Grading adaptations for students with disabilities. *Intervention in School and Clinic, 41,* 87–98.

Spicuzza, R., Ysseldyke, J., Lemkuil, A., Koscioleck, S., Boys, C., & Teelucksingh, E. (2001). Effects of using a curriculum-based monitoring system on the classroom instructional environment and math achievement. *Journal of School Psychology, 39*(6), 521–542.

Stecker, P. M., Fuchs, D., & Fuchs, L. S. (2008). Progress monitoring as essential practice within response to intervention. *Rural Special Education Quarterly, 27*(4), 10–17.

Stiggins, R. J. (1993). Teacher training in assessment: Overcoming the neglect. In S. L. Wise (Ed.), *Teacher training in measurement and assessment skills* (pp. 27–40). Lincoln, NE: Buros Institute of Mental Measurements.

Stiggins, R. J. (2008). *An introduction to student-involved assessment for learning* (5th ed.). Upper Saddle River, NJ: Pearson/Merrill Prentice Hall.

Stiggins, R. J., Frisbie, D. A., & Griswold, P. A. (1989). Inside high school grading practices: Building a research agenda. *Educational Measurement: Issues and Practice, 8*(2), 5–14.

Tomlinson, T. (1992). *Hard work and high expectations: Motivating students to learn*. Washington, DC: Office of Educational Research and Improvement, U.S. Department of Education.

Truog, A. L., & Friedman, S. J. (1996, April). *Evaluating high school teachers' written grading policies from a measurement perspective*. Paper presented at the annual meeting of the National Council on Measurement in Education, New York, NY.

Twain, M. (1888). *Letter to George Bainton*. Retrieved from http://www.twainquotes.com/Lightning.html

Waldron, N. L. (1998). The effects of an inclusive school program on students with mild and severe learning disabilities. *Exceptional Children, 64,* 395–405.

Waltman, K. K., & Frisbie, D. A. (1994). Parents' understanding of their children's report card grades. *Applied Measurement in Education, 7*(3), 223–240.

Wiggins, G. (1996). Honesty and fairness: Toward better grading and reporting. In T. R. Guskey (Ed.), *Communicating student learning: 1996 yearbook of the Association for Supervision and Curriculum Development* (pp. 141–176). Alexandria, VA: Association for Supervision and Curriculum Development.

Willingham, W. W., Pollack, J. M., & Lewis, C. (2002). Grades and test scores: Accounting for observed differences. *Journal of Educational Measurement, 39*(1), 1–37.

Ysseldyke, J. E., Spicuzza, R., Kosciolek, S., & Boys, C. (2003). Effects of a learning information system on mathematics achievement and classroom structure. *Journal of Educational Research, 96*(3), 163–174.

Index

CORWIN

A SAGE Company

The Corwin logo—a raven striding across an open book—represents the union of courage and learning. Corwin is committed to improving education for all learners by publishing books and other professional development resources for those serving the field of PreK–12 education. By providing practical, hands-on materials, Corwin continues to carry out the promise of its motto: **"Helping Educators Do Their Work Better."**